Eleven Year Mathcounts National Competition Solutions

1990 – 2000 Sprint and Target Rounds

http://www.mymathcounts.com/index.php

This is a solution book for 1990 - 2000 Mathcounts National Competition Sprint and Target round problems. The problems attached are for your reference only. To avoid possible copyright issues, we have changed the *wording*, but not the *substance*, of the problems. Please refer to Mathcounts.org for original test problems if you have any question. Please contact mymathcounts@gmail.com for suggestions, corrections, or clarifications of the solutions.

Contributors

Jane Chen, Author, Reviewer.
Sam Chen, Author.
Yongcheng Chen, Ph.D., Author, Reviewer.
Guiling Chen, Owner, mymathcounts.com, Typesetter, Editor

© 2013 mymathcounts.com. All rights reserved. Printed in the United States of America Reproduction of any portion of this book without the written permission of the authors is strictly prohibited, except as may be expressly permitted by the U.S. Copyright Act.

ISBN-13: 978-1492891604
ISBN-10: 1492891606

Table of Contents

1. 1990 National Sprint and Target Round Solutions — 1

2. 1991 National Sprint and Target Round Solutions — 11

3. 1992 National Sprint and Target Round Solutions — 24

4. 1993 National Sprint and Target Round Solutions — 36

5. 1994 National Sprint and Target Round Solutions — 49

6. 1995 National Sprint and Target Round Solutions — 60

7. 1996 National Sprint and Target Round Solutions — 71

8. 1997 National Sprint and Target Round Solutions — 84

9. 1998 National Sprint and Target Round Solutions — 94

10. 1999 National Sprint and Target Round Solutions — 106

11. 2000 National Sprint and Target Round Solutions — 119

Attachment: Problems for 11 sprint and 11 target tests — 133

Index — 188

This page is intentionally left blank.

1990 Mathcounts National Sprint Round Solutions

1. Solution: –2.
Expand $(a+b)^2(a-b)^2 = (a^2-b^2)^2 = a^4 - 2a^2b^2 + b^4$
The coefficient of the a^2b^2 term is –2.

2. Solution: $\dfrac{\sqrt{3}}{3}$.

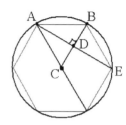

Triangle ABC is an equilateral triangle with AD as its height.
Triangle ABD is a right triangle with angles of degree 30, 60, and 90.

So, $AD = \dfrac{AB}{2}\sqrt{3}$. $\dfrac{AB}{AE} = \dfrac{AB}{2AD} = \dfrac{AB}{2 \times \dfrac{AB}{2}\sqrt{3}} = \dfrac{\sqrt{3}}{3}$.

3. Solution: 100.
Let P represent the amount the shop owner paid to purchase the coat.
The original price of a coat was marked up 50%. So the price was $(1 + 0.5) = 1.5P$.
The price was later reduced by 20%. The price became: $(1 – 0.2) \times 1.5P = 0.8 \times 1.5P$.
Finally the price was reduced an additional 10%. The price became: $(1 – 0.1) \times 0.8 \times 1.5P = 0.9 \times 0.8 \times 1.5P$
The coat was sold for $108: $0.9 \times 0.8 \times 1.5P = 108 \Rightarrow P = \dfrac{108}{1.5 \times 0.9 \times 0.8} = 100$.

4. Solution: 1/64.
There are 4 × 4 × 4 = 64 possible three-digit numbers that can be formed using the digits 1, 3, 5, or 7. Out of all of the numbers formed, only one is the number 111. The probability that a slip of paper contains the number 111 is 1/64.

5. Solution: $\dfrac{480}{11}$.

Let x be the smallest positive fraction that we are looking for.

$x \times \dfrac{11}{60} = x \times \dfrac{11}{2^2 \times 3 \times 5} = 2^3 \quad \Rightarrow \quad x = \dfrac{2^2 \times 3 \times 5 \times 2^3}{11} = \dfrac{480}{11}$

6. Solution: c.
Following the chart above, $(b\nabla(a\nabla d))\nabla(b\nabla c) = (b\nabla d)\nabla a = c\nabla a = c$

1990 Mathcounts National Sprint Round Solutions

7. Solution: $5\frac{5}{6}$.

The harmonic mean of 5 and 7 is $\dfrac{2}{\frac{1}{5}+\frac{1}{7}} = \dfrac{35}{6} = 5\dfrac{5}{6}$

8. Solution: 2163.
Let the 21th term be a_{21} and the sum of the first 21 terms of the series be S. The series is an arithmetic series beginning with 3 with a common difference of 10. So,
$a_{21} = 3+(21-1)\times 10 = 203$.
$S = \dfrac{3+203}{2}\times 21 = 2163$.

9. Solution: 31.
Square both sides: $5n+4 = 169 \rightarrow 5n = 165 \rightarrow n = 31$.

10. Solution: 45.5.
Let the lengths of two legs be $5a$ and $12a$. By the Pythagorean Theorem, the hypotenuse is $\sqrt{(5a)^2+(12a)^2} = 13a$. The perimeter is 105, so
$5a + 12a + 13a = 105 \quad \Rightarrow \quad a = 3.5 \quad \Rightarrow \quad 13a = 45.5$.
The length of the hypotenuse is 45.5.

11. Solution: 91.
$1936 = 44^2$. The next two years that will be perfect squares are the expanded values of 45^2 and 46^2. The positive difference between the two years is $46^2 - 45^2 = (46-45)(46+45) = 91$.

12. Solution: 7.
LCM (21, 24, 60) = LCM (3×7, 3×2^3, $3 \times 2^2 \times 5$). The greatest prime factor is 7.

13. Solution: 56%.
Let the diameter of the original circle be d and the diameter of the new circle be d_1. The increase in area equals

1990 Mathcounts National Sprint Round Solutions

$$\frac{\frac{1}{4}\pi d_1^2 - \frac{1}{4}\pi d^2}{\frac{1}{4}\pi d^2} = (\frac{d_1}{d})^2 - 1 = 1.25^2 - 1 = 0.5625 = 56\%.$$

14. Solution: 10.
$12n - 12 + 5n - 5 - 7n + 7 = x(n-1) \Rightarrow \quad 10(n-1) = x(n-1) \quad \Rightarrow \quad x = 10.$

15. Solution: 3/5.
The given set can be re-written as {0, 1, 1, 64, 1}.
The probability that a randomly chosen element is 1 is 3/5.

16. Solution: 650.
According to the table, for every 40 candies, 13 are yellow. Let x represent the number of yellow candies in 2000 candies. Then,
$$\frac{13}{40} = \frac{x}{2000} \to x = \frac{2000 \times 13}{40} = 650$$

17. Solution: 900.
Let x be the number of students who voted in the election. The number of people who voted for candidate A is $33\frac{1}{3}\% \times x$.
The number of people who voted for candidate B is $\frac{9}{20}x$.
The number of people who voted for candidate C is $\frac{2}{15}x$.
The number of people who voted for candidate D is 75. So,
$33\frac{1}{3}\% \times x + \frac{9}{20}x + \frac{2}{15}x + 75 = x \quad \Rightarrow \quad x = 900.$

18. Solution: 6.
Let x be the number of typed pages and y be the number of hours it takes to type x typed pages. For every five handwritten pages, the typist can produce four typed pages. So,
$\frac{4}{5} = \frac{x}{105} \quad \Rightarrow \quad x = 84.$
The typist can type 14 pages per hour, so

$\dfrac{1}{14} = \dfrac{y}{84}$ $\Rightarrow$ $y = 6$. It takes 6 hours for the typist to type 105 handwritten pages.

19. Solution: 391.

Let the quadratic function be
$$y = ax^2 + bx + c$$
Then,
$$7 = 4a + 2b + c \quad (1)$$
$$17 = 9a + 3b + c \quad (2)$$
$$31 = 16a + 4b + c \quad (3)$$
(2) – (1): $10 = 5a + b$ \quad (4)
(3) – (2): $14 = 7a + b$ \quad (5)
(5) – (4): $a = 2 \Rightarrow b = 0, c = -1$
$y = 2x^2 - 1 = 2 \times 14^2 - 1 = 391$.

20. Solution: 3.
Since $99 = 9 \times 11$, in order for the number to be divisible by 99, the number must be divisible by both 9 and 11.
In order for a number to be divisible by 9, the sum of its digits must be divisible by 9:
$2 + 1 + 3 + 5 + 8 + t + n \equiv 0 \mod 9 \Rightarrow t + n = 8$.
In order for a number to be divisible by 11,
$(n + 8 + 3 + 2) - (t + 5 + 1) \equiv 0 \mod 11$
$\Rightarrow \quad n + 7 - t \equiv 0 \mod 11$
$\Rightarrow \quad n + 7 - (8 - n) \equiv 0 \mod 11$
$\Rightarrow \quad 2n \equiv 1 \mod 11 \quad \Rightarrow \quad n = 6 \text{ and } t = 2.$
$n/t = 3$.

21. Solution: 111,111,111.
The eighth line of the pattern will be
$12345678 \times 9 + 9 = 111{,}111{,}111$.

22. Solution: 84%.
Call the number of sales at the beginning of 1986 x.

1990 Mathcounts National Sprint Round Solutions

After a decrease by 30%, another decrease by 25%, and an increase by 20%, the total sales in 1989 were: $x \times (1 + 33\frac{1}{3}\%) \times 0.7 \times 0.75 \times 1.2 = 0.84x = \frac{84}{100}x$.

Thus, total sales in 1989 were 84% of the sales at the beginning of 1986.

23. Solution: 11/450.

There are $999 - 100 + 1 = 900$ three-digit numbers. There are 22 three-digit perfect squares (the smallest square number is $10^2 = 100$ and the greatest is $31^2 = 961$, $31 - 10 + 1 = 22$).

The probability that a number selected is a perfect square is $22/900 = 11/450$.

24. Solution: 1 and 2.

We re-write the original equation as
$3^{x^2 - 3x} = 3^{-2}$
$\Rightarrow x^2 - 3x = -2$
$\Rightarrow x^2 - 3x + 2 = 0$
$\Rightarrow (x-1)(x-2) = 0 \Rightarrow x = 1$ and $x = 2$.

25. Solution:

$p = \text{LCM}(36, 54) = \text{LCM}(2^2 \times 3^2, 3^3 \times 2) = 2^2 \times 3^3 = 108$
$q = \text{GCF}(36, 54) = \text{GCF}(2^2 \times 3^2, 3^3 \times 2) = 2 \times 3^2 = 18$
$\frac{p-q}{10} = \frac{108 - 18}{10} = 9$.

26. Solution: $1\frac{7}{8}$,

$$\cfrac{1}{\cfrac{2}{\cfrac{3}{\cfrac{4}{5}}}} = \cfrac{1}{\cfrac{2}{\cfrac{3}{\frac{4}{5}}}} = \cfrac{1}{\cfrac{2}{\frac{15}{4}}} = \cfrac{1}{\frac{8}{15}} = \frac{15}{8} = 1\frac{7}{8}$$

27. Solution: 120.

Using the distance formula, the length between points Q and R is

$QR = \sqrt{(2+2)^2 + (-4-4)^2} = \sqrt{80} = 4\sqrt{5}$.
The length between RS is
$RS = \sqrt{QS^2 - QR^2} = \sqrt{4 \times 65 - 80} = \sqrt{180} = 6\sqrt{5}$
The area of the rectangle = $RS \times QR = 6\sqrt{5} \times 4\sqrt{5} = 120$.

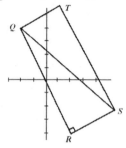

28. Solution: $4.25.
From the diagram below, we see that the second daughter received $3 from her father. She needs $6.25 – 3 = $4.25 to purchase a T-shirt.

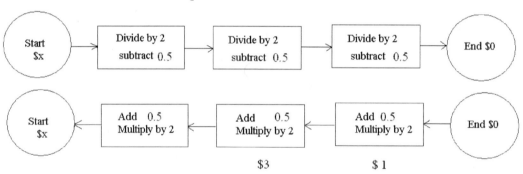

Answer: $4.25.

29. Solution: 45.
Any two points will form one line. The maximum number of distinct lines that can be formed by 10 points is $\binom{10}{2} = 45$.

30. Solution: 6.
$6\sqrt{(x-1)(x-2)(x-3)} = 0$. After dividing both sides by 6 and squaring the results, we get $(x-1)(x-2)(x-3) = 0$
The solutions to this equations are $x = 1$, $x = 2$, and $x = 3$. The sum is $1 + 2 + 3 = 6$.

1990 Mathcounts National Competition Target Round Solutions

1. Solution: 87.
Method 1:
When she stacks them by elevens, ten are left over. So she may have 21, 332, 43, 54, 65, 76, 87, 98,... disks.

When she stacks them by tens, seven are left over. So she may have 17, 27, 37, 47, 57, 67, 77, 87, 97,… disks.

when she stacks them by sixes, three are left over. So she may have 9, 15, 21, 27, 33, 39, 45, 51, 57, 63, 69, 75, 81, 87, 93,…… disks.

The least common multiple is 87.

Method 2:
Let n be the number of disks that Amy has. According to the problem,
$n \equiv 10 \quad \text{Mod } 11$ (1)
$n \equiv 7 \quad \text{Mod } 10$ (2)
$n \equiv 3 \quad \text{Mod } 6$ (3)

For (2) and (3), we have:

$n + 3 \equiv 0 \quad \text{Mod } 10$ (4)
$n + 3 \equiv 0 \quad \text{Mod } 6$ (5)

Since the LCM (10, 6) = 30, (4) and (5) become:

$n + 3 \equiv 0 \quad \text{Mod } 30$ (6)

n can be 27, 57, or 87. Among these three integers, only $87 \equiv 10 \text{ Mod } 11$. Amy has 87 disks.

2. Solution: $\frac{7}{4}$.

In order for the relationship to not become a function, we set:
$$-2m + 1 = -6m + 8 \Rightarrow 4m = 7 \Rightarrow m = \frac{7}{4}.$$

Note: If you confuse the domain with the range of a function, here's a good way to decide a given relation is a function or not:

1990 Mathcounts National Competition Target Round Solutions

The items (x) and the prices (y) in a store form a function relationship. The function's domain is the items in the store, and the range is the price of the item. Every item in the store has a price, but no item has two different prices attached to it. You can have several different items with the same price.

3. Solution: $\frac{1}{12}$.

We have 36 possible outcomes and three of them, as shown below in the table, are 8. The probability that the sum of the numbers showing is 8 is $P = \frac{3}{36} = \frac{1}{12}$.

	1	2	3	4	5	6
2	3	4	5	6	7	8
4	5	6	7	8	9	10
6	7	8	9	10	11	12
8	9	10	11	12	13	14
10	11	12	13	14	15	16
12	13	14	15	16	17	18

4. Solution: $24\sqrt{2}$.

Let a be the side length and d_1 be the diagonal length of the smaller square.
Let $a + 4$ be the side length and d_2 be the diagonal length of the larger square. The area of the smaller square is 48 square inches less than the area of the larger, so
$(a+4)^2 = a^2 + 48 \Rightarrow a^2 + 8a + 16 = a^2 + 48 \Rightarrow 8a = 32 \Rightarrow a = 4$.
$d_1 = 4\sqrt{2}$ and $d_2 = 8\sqrt{2}$.
So the sum of the lengths of all the diagonals of both squares is $2(d_1 + d_2) = 2(4\sqrt{2} + 8\sqrt{2}) = 24\sqrt{2}$.

5. Solution: 4 and all integers less than −1.
Step 1: Find the roots of the equation: $(x - 3)(x + 1)(x - 5) = 0$.

$x = 3$, $x = -1$, and $x = 5$.

Step 2: Mark these points on the number line:

1990 Mathcounts National Competition Target Round Solutions

Step 3: Draw a curve in this fashion:
Start from the upper right of the number line above the maximum root (in this case, 5), and go down below the number line and go up through 3. Continue to go above the number line to –1. Then go down below the number line through –1. See the figure below for an image.

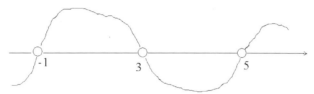

Step 4: Mark the regions with "+" and "–" signs. If the region is above the number line, mark the region with a "+" sign. Otherwise mark a "–" sign.

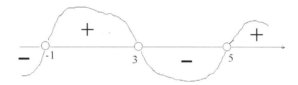

Since $(x-3)(x+1)(x-5) < 0$, we are looking for the regions that have a "–" sign. The solutions to this inequality will be:
$-3 < x < 5$ and $x < -1$.

6. Solution: $\dfrac{1+\sqrt{5}}{2}$.

Let x be the length of the rectangle.
$$\dfrac{1}{x} = \dfrac{x}{1+x} \quad \Rightarrow \quad x^2 - x - 1 = 0$$
This is a quadratic equation and we use the Quadratic formula to solve for x.
$$x_1 = \dfrac{1+\sqrt{5}}{2} \text{ and } x_2 = \dfrac{1-\sqrt{5}}{2}.$$

The second solution is extraneous since the length of a rectangle could not be negative.
So the length of a golden rectangle with the width of 1 inch is $\dfrac{1+\sqrt{5}}{2}$ inches.

1990 Mathcounts National Competition Target Round Solutions

7. Solution: $\frac{2}{9}$.

We want to find the ratio of the area that is shaded in the figure to the area of the large circle.

$$Ratio = \frac{\pi \times 3^2 - \pi \times 1^2}{\pi \times 6^2} = \frac{2}{9}.$$

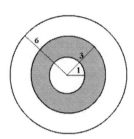

8. Solution: 16.

Step 1: Since we want to get the maximum number of regions, we cut the circle in such a way that no line will go through the same point. There are $m = 11$ regions, as shown in the left figure.

Step 2: In order to obtain the minimum number of regions, we cut the circle in such a way so that no lines intersect. There are $n = 5$ regions, as shown in the right figure.
$m + n = 16.$

1991 Mathcounts National Sprint Round Solution

1. Solution: 243.
$2^a = 32 = 2^5 \Rightarrow a = 5.$
$a^b = 125 = 5^3 \Rightarrow b = 3.$
$b^a = 3^5 = 243.$

2. Solution: 0.
Add $x + 3$ to both sides of the inequality. The inequality becomes
$4x + x < 5 \Rightarrow x < 1.$ Thus 0 is the greatest whole number that will satisfy the inequality.

3. Solution: 4.
The number of beakers of water that will be able to fill the tank is equivalent to the number of times the volume of the cylindrical beaker will go into the volume of the spherical tank.
$$\frac{\frac{4}{3}\pi R^3}{\pi r^2 h} = \frac{\frac{4}{3} \times 6^3}{3^2 \times 8} = 4.$$

4. Solution: 49.
Square both sides of the equation, we get:
$1 + \sqrt{2 + \sqrt{n}} = 4$
$\Rightarrow \sqrt{2 + \sqrt{n}} = 3$
$\Rightarrow 2 + \sqrt{n} = 9$
$\Rightarrow \sqrt{n} = 7 \Rightarrow n = 49.$

5. Solution: 52.
The total height of five old buildings is equal to $625 + a + b + c + 858 = 733 \times 5$.
The total height of the five new buildings is equal to
$(a + b + c + 858) + 885 = (733 \times 5 - 625) + 885.$
The amount of increase in the mean height of the five buildings in feet is equal to
$\frac{733 \times 5 + 885 - 625}{5} - 733 = 785 - 733 = 52.$

6. Solution: 25.
The geometric mean of two numbers is the square root of the product.

1991 Mathcounts National Sprint Round Solution

$$\sqrt{6\frac{1}{4} \times 100} = \sqrt{\frac{25}{4} \times 100} = \frac{5 \times 10}{2} = 25.$$

7. Solution: $4\frac{1}{4}$.

$$\frac{n}{m} + \frac{m}{n} = \frac{n^2 + m^2}{nm} = \frac{n^2 + m^2 - 2nm + 2nm}{nm} = \frac{(n-m)^2}{nm} + 2$$

We want $n - m$ to be as large as possible and $n \times m$ to be as small as possible in order to achieve the greatest value for $\frac{n}{m} + \frac{m}{n}$. When $n - m$ is as large as possible, $n \times m$ is as small as possible as well, so we only need to focus on making the subtraction as large as possible.

The largest value of $n - m$ is $80 - 20 = 60$. The greatest value for $\frac{n}{m} + \frac{m}{n}$ is

$$\frac{(n-m)^2}{nm} + 2 = \frac{60^2}{80 \times 20} + 2 = \frac{9}{4} + 2 = 4\frac{1}{4}.$$

8. Solution: 36.

Method 1: Adding all of the equations together, we have: $1^3 + 2^3 + 3^3 + \ldots + 6^3 = n^2$
We know that

$$1^3 + 2^3 + 3^3 + \ldots + 6^3 = [\frac{(1+6)6}{2}]^2 = 21^2, \quad n^2 = 21^2 \Rightarrow \quad n = 21$$

$$m^2 = 21^2 - 6^3 = 441 - 216 = 225 \quad \Rightarrow \quad m = 15$$

$m + n = 21 + 15 = 36$

Note: $1^3 + 2^3 + 3^3 + \ldots + n^3 = [\frac{(1+n)n}{2}]^2$

Method 2: We observe some patterns that we can use to derive n and m:

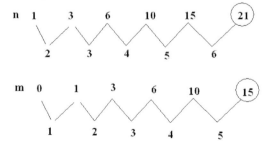

$n + m = 21 + 15 = 36$

1991 Mathcounts National Sprint Round Solution

9. Solution: 10.
We like to find the difference between the largest and smallest prime factors of 15,015.
$15015 = 15 \times 1001 = 3 \times 5 \times 7 \times 11 \times 13$
The largest prime factor of 15,015 is 13 and the smallest is 3. The difference between the two is $13 - 3 = 10$.

Note: $1001 = 7 \times 11 \times 13$.

10. Solution: $4\sqrt{3}$.

The length of $\overline{OA} = \sqrt{x^2 + y^2} = \sqrt{x^2 + (-\frac{1}{2}x^2)^2} = \sqrt{x^2 + \frac{1}{4}x^4}$.

The length of $\overline{AB} = 2x$.
Since the triangle is equilateral, $\overline{OA} = \overline{AB}$, or
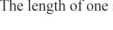$= 2x$.

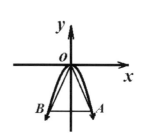

Squaring both sides of the equation above, we have:
$x^2 + \frac{1}{4}x^4 = 4x^2 \rightarrow 1 + \frac{1}{4}x^2 = 4 \rightarrow x = 2\sqrt{3}$..
The length of one side of the triangle is $2x = 2 \times 2\sqrt{3} = 4\sqrt{3}$.

11. Solution: 120.
A phonograph record makes 33 1/3 revolutions in 60 seconds. We need to figure out how many revolutions it will make in $3 \times 60 + 36$ seconds.

$$\frac{33\frac{1}{3}}{60} = \frac{x}{180 + 36} \Rightarrow x = 120.$$

12. Solution: 15.
In order to find the maximum number of discs that can be purchased, we want to have as many packs of 4 as possible, because that is the cheapest.
$130 = 33.25 \times 3 + 17.75 \times 1 + 10.79 \times 1 + R$
The maximum number of discs that can be purchased with 130 dollars is 3 packs of 4, 1 pack of 2, and 1 disc, or
$3 \times 4 + 1 \times 2 + 1 = 15$.

13. Solution: 5000 gallons
Let V be the total number of gallons the tank holds.

1991 Mathcounts National Sprint Round Solution

$0.26V + 700 = 0.4V \to 700 = 0.4V - 0.26V \to 0.14V = 700 \to V = 5{,}000.$

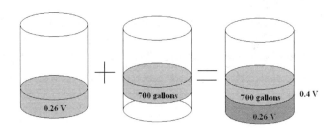

14. Solution: 8.

We know that $1^3 + 2^3 + 3^3 + \ldots + n^3 = [\dfrac{(1+n)n}{2}]^2$

And $1 + 2 + 3 + \ldots + n = \dfrac{(1+n)n}{2}$. So,

$$\dfrac{1^3 + 2^3 + 3^3 + \ldots + n^3}{1 + 2 + 3 + \ldots + n} = \dfrac{[\dfrac{(1+n)n}{2}]^2}{\dfrac{(1+n)n}{2}} = \dfrac{(1+n)n}{2}.$$

$\dfrac{(1+n)n}{2} = 36 \to n^2 + n - 72 = 0 \to (n-8)(n+9) = 0 \to n = 8.$

15. Solution: 56.

The first car traveled 7 hours at the speed of 40 miles per hour when the second car overtook it within 5 hours of travelling at the speed of x miles per hour. The distances traveled by both cars are the same, so by the distance-rate formula,
$7 \times 40 = 5 \times x \implies x = 56$ miles per hour.

16. Solution: 3.

We are asked to find the units digits of the sum of all the integers from 100 to 202.
Method 1:

There are total $202 - 100 + 1 = 103$ numbers from 100 to 202 inclusive. So $n = 103$.
The sum of them is $S = \dfrac{(a_1 + a_n)}{2} = \dfrac{(100 + 202) \times 103}{2} = 151 \times 103$.
Since we only care about the units digits, so it 3.

Method 2:

1991 Mathcounts National Sprint Round Solution

Because we are focusing on the units digit of the sum, we can take "mod 10" of the sum, which eliminates all other unwanted digits.
$100 + 101 + 102 +\ldots + 202 \equiv 0 + 1 + 2 +\ldots 8 + 9 + 0 + 1 + 2 \pmod{10}$
There are total $202 - 100 + 1 = 103$ numbers from 100 to 202 inclusive, so we have
$100+101+102+\ldots+ 202 \equiv (0 + 1 + 2 +\ldots+9) \times 10 + 0 + 1 + 2 = 0 + 1 + 2 = 3 \pmod{10}$
The units digit is 3.

17. Solution: 10.
Let P_A represent the probability of earning an A.
Let P_B represent the probability of earning a B.
Let P_C represent the probability of earning a C.
Since the probability of earning an A is 0.7 times the probability of earning a B,
$P_A = 0.7P_B$.
The probability of earning a C is 1.4 times the probability of earning a B, or
$P_C = 1.4P_B$.
All grades are A, B, or C, so
$P_A + P_B + P_C = 1$.
Substituting the necessary values,
$0.7P_B + P_B + 1.4P_B = 1 \rightarrow 3.1P_B = 1 \rightarrow P_B = \dfrac{1}{3.1} = \dfrac{10}{31}$. There are 10 students who earned a B among the 31 total students.

18. Solution: $x^2 + y^2 = 13$.

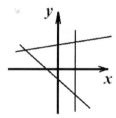

Method 1: The points of intersection of the lines can be found by setting the three lines equivalent to each other. We calculate the points of intersection as $A(2, 3)$, $B(2, -3)$, and $C(-3, 2)$.
Let the center of the circle be $O(x, y)$. Using the distance formula, we have:

$\overline{OA} = \overline{OB}$: $\sqrt{(x-2)^2 + (y-3)^2} = \sqrt{(x-2)^2 + (y+3)^2}$ (1)

$\overline{OA} = \overline{OC}$: $\sqrt{(x-2)^2 + (y-3)^2} = \sqrt{(x+3)^2 + (y-3)^2}$ (2)

Squaring both sides of (1) and (2), we get:
$(x-2)^2 + (y-3)^2 = (x-2)^2 + (y+3)^2$ (3)
$(x-2)^2 + (y-3)^2 = (x+3)^2 + (y-2)^2$ (4)

From (3), we have: $(y-3)^2 = (y+3)^2 \Rightarrow y = 0$.

1991 Mathcounts National Sprint Round Solution

Substituting $y = 0$ into (4):
$(x-2)^2 + 3^2 = (x+3)^2 + 2^2 \to x^2 - 4x + 4 + 9 = x^2 + 6x + 9 + 4 \to 10x = 0 \to x = 0.$
Thus, the center of the circle is at the origin and the radius of the circle is
$$\overline{OA} = \sqrt{(x-2)^2 + (y-3)^2} = \sqrt{2^2 + 3^2} = \sqrt{13}$$
The equation is of the circle is then $x^2 + y^2 = 13$.

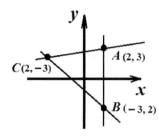

Method 2:
We know that the equation of the circles passing thorugh two points (x_1, y_1) and (x_2, y_2) is
$(x-x_1)(x-x_2) + (y-y_1)(y-y_2) + k[(x-x_1)(y_2-y_1) - (y-y_1)(x_2-x_1)] = 0$, where k is a parameter.
With two points $(2, 3)$, $(2, -3)$, we then have
$(x-2)(x-2) + (y-3)(y+3) + k[(x-2)(-3-3) - (y-3)(2-2)] = 0 \Rightarrow$
$x^2 - 4x + 4 + y^2 - 9 - 6k(x-2) = 0$.
Since the circle also passes through the points $(-3, 2)$, we get
$(-3)^2 - 4(-3) + 4 + 2^2 - 9 - 6k(-3-2) = 0 \Rightarrow \quad 20 + 30k = 0 \Rightarrow \quad k = -\dfrac{2}{3}$

The equation of the circle is $x^2 - 4x + 4 + y^2 - 9 - 6(-\dfrac{2}{3})(x-2) = 0 \Rightarrow x^2 + y^2 = 13$.

Method 3:
The general form of a circle is $x^2 + y^2 + Dx + Ey + F = 0$.
For the point $(2, 3)$, we have
$2^2 + 3^2 + 2D + 3E + F = 0 \qquad \Rightarrow \qquad 2D + 3E + F = -13 \quad (1)$
For the point $(2, -3)$, we have
$2^2 + (-3)^2 + 2D - 3E + F = 0 \qquad \Rightarrow \qquad 2D - 3E + F = -13 \quad (2)$
For the point $(-3, 2)$. we have
$3^2 + (-2)^2 + 3D - 2E + F = 0 \qquad \Rightarrow \qquad 3D - 2E + F = -13 \quad (3)$

$(1) - (2):\ 6E = 0 \qquad \Rightarrow \qquad E = 0 \qquad (4)$
Solving the system of equations (1) and (3) considering $E = 0$:
$D = 0$ and $F = -13$.
The equation of the circle is $x^2 + y^2 - 13 = 0$ or $x^2 + y^2 = 13$.

19. Solution: 170%.

1991 Mathcounts National Sprint Round Solution

After the size of the image is increased by 80% and 50%, it becomes 1.8×1.5 times its size, or $1.8 \times 1.5 = 2.7 = 1 + \frac{170}{100}$. The percent increase when two lenses are used together in the image is 170%.

20. Solution: 155.
We are given that n is a prime number. We are asked to find the smallest composite number in the form of $n^2 - n - 1$.

$n^2 - n - 1 = (n-1) \times n - 1$. Note that n is a prime number. After plugging in prime numbers, we get
$2 \times 3 - 1 = 5$; $4 \times 5 - 1 = 19$; $6 \times 7 - 1 = 41$; $10 \times 11 - 1 = 109$; $12 \times 13 - 1 = 155$.
155 is the smallest composite number produced by $n^2 - n - 1$.

21. Solution: 45.
Let the five odd consecutive integers be

$2x + 1$, $2x + 3$, $2x + 5$, $2x + 7$, and $2x + 9$.

The sum of the five integers equals $10x + 25 = 5(2x + 5) = N^2$.

5 and another square number must be the factors of $2x + 5$ in order for the product of 5 and $2x + 5$ to be a perfect square, or
$2x + 5 = 5 \times n^2$ or
$N^2 = 25 \times n^2$.
The smallest value for n is 1 (in this case x = 0), which gives $N^2 = 25$. However, this is the case given in the problem, so we need to keep on looking.
The second smallest value for n is 2, which does not work because x isn't an integer.
The third smallest value for n is 3 (in this case x = 20), which gives $N^2 = 225$.
The median of the set is 225/5 = 45.

22. Solution: 50.
Let the width of the rectangle be x.
The area of the rectangle equals $A = x \times 2x = 2x^2$
We know that the length of the diagonal is $5\sqrt{5}$, or
$x^2 + (2x)^2 = (5\sqrt{5})^2 \rightarrow 5x^2 = 25 \times 5 \rightarrow x^2 = 25 \rightarrow A = 50$.

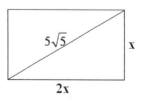

23. Solution: $\sqrt{6}$.
Looking at the figure below, the length of CB is $3\sqrt{2}$.

$\triangle ACB$ and $\triangle AFG$ are similar to each other because they share an angle and both have right angles, so

$\dfrac{6}{3\sqrt{2}} = \dfrac{1}{FG} \quad \Rightarrow \quad FG = \dfrac{\sqrt{2}}{2}$. Using the Pythagorean Theorem on $\triangle AFG$, we get $AG = \sqrt{1^2 + (\dfrac{\sqrt{2}}{2})^2} = \dfrac{\sqrt{6}}{2}$.

$\triangle ADE$ and $\triangle AFG$ are also similar to each other because they share an angle and both have right angles, so

$\dfrac{1}{AG} = \dfrac{2}{x} \quad \Rightarrow \quad x = \sqrt{6}$.

The length of the portion of segment AB that is contained in the center cube is $\sqrt{6}$.

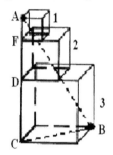
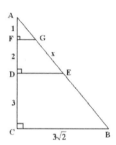

24. Solution: 640.
Let the number be x. Since the positive integer has a square root between 25 and 25.3, we have
$25 < \sqrt{x} < 25.3$

Squaring both sides, we get $625 < x < 640.09$ or $624 \leq x \leq 640$.

We also know that the positive integer is also divisible by 14. We see that 630 is in between 624 and 650, so it has a square root between 25 and 25.3, and is divisible by 14.

25. Solution: 54.
We know that 330 people can construct 30 km of railway track in 9 months. Let t be the number of months for 275 people to construct 150 km of track.

$\dfrac{km}{\# ppl \times \# months} = \dfrac{30}{330 \times 9} = \dfrac{150}{275 \times t} \rightarrow t = \dfrac{150 \times 330 \times 9}{30 \times 275} \Rightarrow t = 54.$

1991 Mathcounts National Sprint Round Solution

26. Solution: $\dfrac{211}{36}$.

The expression $(1\frac{1}{2})^{-2}+(1\frac{1}{2})^{-1}+(1\frac{1}{2})^{0}+(1\frac{1}{2})^{1}+(1\frac{1}{2})^{2}$ is equivalent to

$\dfrac{4}{9}+\dfrac{2}{3}+1+\dfrac{3}{2}+\dfrac{9}{4}=4+\dfrac{4}{9}+\dfrac{1}{2}+\dfrac{1}{4}=4+\dfrac{67}{36}=\dfrac{211}{36}$.

27. Solution: 1.

$1+\dfrac{1}{\dfrac{2x+3}{2x}}=\dfrac{7}{5} \Rightarrow \dfrac{2x}{2x+3}=\dfrac{2}{5} \Rightarrow 10x=4x+6 \Rightarrow x=1.$

28. Solution: 12.
Let V be the speed of the man.

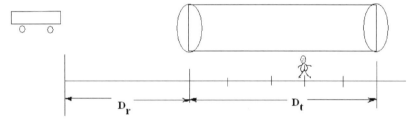

Using the distance-rate formula, when the man runs backwards, we get the ratio:

$\dfrac{D_r}{60}=\dfrac{\frac{3}{5}D_t}{V}$ (1)

Using the distance-rate formula, when the man runs forwards, we get the ratio:

$\dfrac{D_r+D_t}{60}=\dfrac{\frac{2}{5}D_t}{V}$ (2)

Substituting (1) into (2), we get

$\dfrac{\frac{3}{5}D_t}{V}+\dfrac{D_t}{60}=\dfrac{\frac{2}{5}D_t}{V} \Rightarrow \dfrac{3}{5V}+\dfrac{1}{60}=\dfrac{2}{5V} \Rightarrow \dfrac{1}{5V}=\dfrac{1}{60} \Rightarrow V=12.$

1991 Mathcounts National Sprint Round Solution

29. Solution: 1900.
Let x be the weight of the tanker when it is empty and y be the total weight of the water when the tanker is full.
$0.25y + x = 2500$ and $0.75y + x = 3700$.
Subtract the two equations and solve for y and we get $y = 2400$.
Substituting y into an above equation, we can find the value of x.
$x = 1900$.

30. Solution: $5\sqrt{5}$.
We know that $AB = BC = 5$ and $FB = 3$. By the Pythagorean Theorem, $FC = 4$.
$AC = \sqrt{4^2 + 8^2} = \sqrt{80} = 4\sqrt{5}$.
$\Delta AFC \sim \Delta DAB$ ($\angle EAB + \angle EBA = 90°$, $\angle ADB + \angle EBA = 90°$, so ($\angle EAB = \angle ADB = \alpha$).
Therefore,

$$\frac{4}{4\sqrt{5}} = \frac{5}{l} \quad \Rightarrow \quad l = 5\sqrt{5}$$

1991 Mathcounts National Target Round Solutions

1. Solution: 28%.
We want to find the percent of all three-digit numbers contains the digit 5 at least once.
There are $\underline{9} \times \underline{10} \times \underline{10} = 900$ total three-digit numbers.

For any three-digit positive integer without a digit 5 in it, we have 8 choices for the hundreds digit (1, 2, 3, 4, 6, 7, 8, 9), 9 choices for the tens digit (0, 1, 2, 3, 4, 6, 7, 8, 9), and 9 choices for the units digit (0, 1, 2, 3, 4, 6, 7, 8, 9). So there are $\underline{8} \times \underline{9} \times \underline{9} = 648$ three-digit numbers do not contain the digit 5.

The percent of all three-digit numbers that contains the digit 5 at least once is
$\dfrac{900-648}{900} = 28\%$.

2. Solution: 2y.
We are given that the arithmetic mean of an odd number of consecutive odd integers is y.
We like to find the sum of the smallest and largest of the integers.
Let the smallest integer be a and the largest integer be b.
The arithmetic mean of the group of numbers is $\dfrac{a+b}{2} = y \to a + b = 2y$.
The sum of the smallest and largest of the integers is $2y$.

3. Solution: 8.
We are asked to find the 100th digit of the decimal representation of $\dfrac{1}{7}$. We know that
$\dfrac{1}{7} = 0.\overline{142857}$.

The sequence 142857 repeats itself every 6 digits in the decimal representation of $\dfrac{1}{7}$. The remainder of 100 when it is divided by 6 is $100 - 6 \times 16 = 4$.
The 100th digit is 4th digit of the sequence, which is 8.

4. Solution: $\dfrac{2\sqrt{3}}{3}$.

Connect AD. Extend BF to meet AD. F is the centroid of triangle ABD, since C is the midpoint of BD and E is the midpoint of AB. The centriod divides the triangle into six smaller triangles, which have the same area.

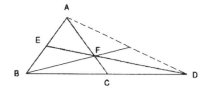

21

1991 Mathcounts National Target Round Solutions

$$S_{BEFC} = \frac{2}{3} S_{\triangle ABC} = \frac{2}{3} \frac{\sqrt{3}}{4} a^2 = \frac{2}{3} \frac{\sqrt{3}}{4} 2^2 = \frac{2\sqrt{3}}{3}.$$

5. Solution: 144.

Let x be the length of the train and v be the speed of the train.

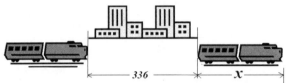

Since it takes 10 seconds for the end of the train to be even with the other end of the station after the front of the train to reaches the station, by the distance-rate formula, $\frac{x+336}{v} = 10 \to x + 336 = 10v$. Since it takes 3 seconds for the train to travel its own length,

$\frac{x}{v} = 3 \to x = 3v$. Substituting this into the previous equation gives

$3v + 336 = 10v \to 7v = 336 \to v = 48$
$x = 144$ (feet).

6. Solution: 30.

$2^{12} - 2^{11} + 2^{10} - 2^9 + \ldots + 2^2 - 2^1$ can be regrouped as
$(2^{12} - 2^{11}) + (2^{10} - 2^9) + \ldots + (2^2 - 2^1)$
$= 2^{11} + 2^9 + 2^7 + 2^5 + 2^3 + 2^1 = 2(2^{10} + 2^8 + 2^6 + 2^4 + 2^2 + 1)$
$= 2(1024 + 256 + 64 + 16 + 1) = 2 \times 1361 = 2 \times 3 \times 5 \times 7 \times 13$.
The sum of the prime factors of the number is $2 + 3 + 5 + 7 + 13 = 30$.

7. Solution: $\frac{3}{5}$.

Let Q, D, N be quarter, dime, or nickel of the coin selected.

Method 1.
Direct way:

The total number of possible ways to pick two coins from six is $\binom{6}{2} = 15$.

Favorable outcomes:

Case I: Q   N $\binom{2}{1}\binom{2}{1} = 4$ ways

Case II: Q   D $\binom{2}{1}\binom{2}{1} = 4$ ways

Case III: Q   Q $\binom{2}{2} = 1$ way

The probability is: $P = \dfrac{Favorable}{Total} = \dfrac{9}{15} = \dfrac{3}{5}$.

Method 2.
Indirect way:

Total outcomes: $\binom{6}{2} = 15$

Unfavorable outcomes:

Case I: N   N $\binom{2}{2} = 1$ way

Case II: D   D $\binom{2}{2} = 1$ way

Case III: N   D $\binom{2}{1}\binom{2}{1} = 4$ ways

The probability is: $P = 1 - \dfrac{6}{15} = 1 - \dfrac{2}{5} = \dfrac{3}{5}$.

8. Solution:
We are given a regular octagon with the side length of 12 cm as shown in the figure. We like to find the length for *BE*.
Draw *CH* such that *CH* is perpendicular to *BE* at *H*. The interior angle of an octagon is 135 degrees.
So, $\angle BCD = 135°$.
$\angle HCD = 90°$, $\angle 1 = \angle 2 = 45°$ and $BH = HC$.
We know that $BC = CD = 12$.
Using the Pythagorean Theorem, $BH = HC = 6\sqrt{2}$.
The area of the trapezoid *BCDE* is
$\dfrac{(12 + 12 + 2 \times 6\sqrt{2})}{2} \times 6\sqrt{2} = 72 + 72\sqrt{2}$.

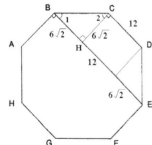

1992 Mathcounts National Sprint Round Solution

1. Solution: 50,000.
Let the amount of the estate at the beginning be x. After Andrea received 20% of her estate, the remaining amount of estate is 0.8x. After her mother received 50% of the remaining, the amount of estate left was $0.8 \times 0.5x = 20{,}000$. $x = 50{,}000$. Below is a chart that sums up our solution.

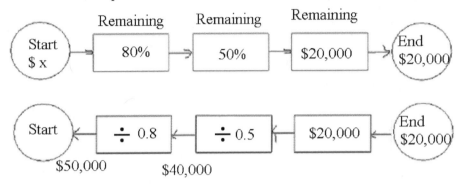

2. Solution: $\dfrac{5}{3}$.

Let $AE = x$. Since $AB = 5$, $EB = 5 - x$.
The area of square $ABCD$ is 5^2 and the area of the shaded region can be found by subtracting the area of the two right triangles from the area of the square.

$$5 \times 5 - \dfrac{2 \times (5-x)^2}{2} = \dfrac{5}{9} \times 5^2 \Rightarrow x = \dfrac{5}{3}.$$

$AE = AF = \dfrac{5}{3}.$

3. Solution: 1.

$a_2 + a_3 + a_4 = 3 \Rightarrow 4 + a_3 - 2 = 3 \Rightarrow a_3 = 1$

$a_{16} + a_{17} + a_{18} = a_{15} + a_{16} + a_{17} \Rightarrow a_{18} = a_{15}$

$a_{13} + a_{14} + a_{15} = a_{12} + a_{13} + a_{14} \Rightarrow a_{15} = a_{12}$

$a_{10} + a_{11} + a_{12} = a_9 + a_{10} + a_{11} \Rightarrow a_{12} = a_9,$

Similarly, $a_9 = a_6 = a_3$ or $a_{18} = a_3 = 1$.

4. Solution: 210.
$y: 22, 21, 20, \ldots, 3$
$x: 20, 19, 18, \ldots, 1$

1992 Mathcounts National Sprint Round Solution

When $y = 22$, x can be 20, 19, ...1. There are 20 pairs: (20, 22,); (19, 22); ...(1, 22).
When $y = 21$, x can be 19, 18, ...1. There are 19 pairs: (19, 21); (18, 21);...(1, 22).
When $y = 20$, x can be 18, 17, ...1. There are 18 pairs: (18, 20); (17, 20);...(1, 22).
...
When $y = 3$, x can be 1. There is 1 pair: (1, 3).
There are a total of $20 + 19 + 18 + ... + 1 = \dfrac{(1+20) \times 20}{2} = 210$ pairs.

5. Solution: –5.
$(x+5)(x^2 - x - 11) - (x+5) = 0$
$\Rightarrow \quad (x+5)(x^2 - x - 11 - 1) = 0$
$\Rightarrow \quad (x+5)(x^2 - x - 12) = 0$
$\Rightarrow \quad (x+5)(x-4)(x+3) = 0$
There are 3 solutions: $x = -3$, $x = -5$, and $x = 4$. The smallest one is $x = -5$.

6. Solution: 2.
Stacey can complete one job in six hours, so can trim the shrubbery at the rate of 1/6. Similarly, her father can trim the shrubbery at the rate of 1/5. Working together, they can trim the shrubbery at the rate of $\dfrac{1}{6} + \dfrac{1}{5}$. Let t denote the number of hours Stacy and her father worked together. Then,

$t \times (\dfrac{1}{6} + \dfrac{1}{5}) = \dfrac{11}{15} \qquad \Rightarrow \qquad t = \dfrac{\frac{11}{15}}{\frac{1}{6} + \frac{1}{5}} = 2$.

They worked together for 2 hours.

7. Solution: 3.
Since there are only two white chips, the number of arrangements is fully determined by the ways that the 5 red chips be separated by these two white chips.
$5 = 5 + 0 = 4 + 1 = 3 + 2$. Hence there are 3 ways, as shown below.

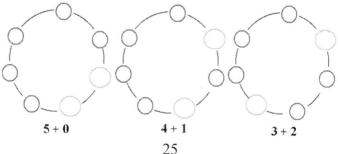

5 + 0   4 + 1   3 + 2

1992 Mathcounts National Sprint Round Solution

8. Solution: 11.
Let the three consecutive positive integers be $x-1$, x, and $x+1$.
$$\frac{(x-1)x(x+1)}{x-1+x+x+1} = 33 \Rightarrow \frac{(x-1)x(x+1)}{3x} = 33 \Rightarrow x^2 - 1 = 99 \Rightarrow$$
$(x-1)(x+1) = 99 = 9 \times 11$.
$x = 10$. The largest of the three integers is 11.

9. Solution:
$10(3^2 - 1) - 5(4^2 - 1) = 80 - 75 = 5$.

10. Solution: $\frac{1}{3}$.

The sum of all the numbers on the die is 21.
Case I: If the bottom face has 5 and top face has 3, then the sum of the numbers on the four lateral faces is $21 - 8 = 13$.
Case II: If the bottom face has 6 and top face has 1, then the sum of the numbers on the four lateral faces is $21 - 7 = 14$.
Case III: If the bottom face has 4 and top face has 2, then the sum of the numbers on the four lateral faces is $21 - 6 = 15$.
The probability that the sum of the numbers on the four lateral faces is a prime number is $\frac{1}{3}$.

11. Solution: $\frac{1023}{1024}$.

The above expression is a geometric sequence with the common ratio $r = \frac{1}{2}$.

The sum of the sequence is $S = \frac{a_1(1-q^n)}{1-q} = \frac{\frac{1}{2}\left(1-(\frac{1}{2})^{10}\right)}{1-\frac{1}{2}} = 1 - \left(\frac{1}{2}\right)^{10} = \frac{1023}{1024}$.

12. Solution: 5.
$2^{40} \equiv 2^4 \equiv 16 \equiv 6 \mod 10$. The units digit of $2^{40} - 1$ is then $6 - 1 = 5$.

13. Solution: 5.

1992 Mathcounts National Sprint Round Solution

We are finding the number of integers x such that:
$|x-1|<3$.
The above inequality becomes the following two inequalities.
$x-1<3 \quad \Rightarrow \quad x<4$
$x-1>-3 \quad \Rightarrow \quad x>-2$
There are a total of 5 integer values in between -2 and 4.

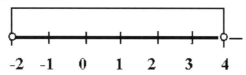

14. Solution: 1.
$m+n>50 \quad \Rightarrow \quad m+n>50 \quad \Rightarrow \quad m+n+10\geq 50-n \quad \Rightarrow \quad n>20$
$m-n\leq 10 \quad \quad\quad 10\geq m-n$
The smallest value for n is then 21.

15. Solution: 16.
Let Daryl's current age be x. In eight years before he is twice as old as he is now, Daryl will be $2x-8$.

Now	8 years before he is twice as old as he is now	Twice as old as he is now
x	$2x-8$	$2x$

$x=\dfrac{2}{3}(2x-8) \Rightarrow \quad x=16$.

16. Solution: 36°.
One interior angle of the regular 20-gons is $\dfrac{(n-2)\times 180°}{n}=\dfrac{(20-2)\times 180°}{20}=162°$.
$\angle ABC$ is equal to two times the interior angle of the regular 20-gon subtracted from 180 degrees, as shown in the figure below.
The desired solution is then $2\times(180°-162°)=2\times 18°=36°$.

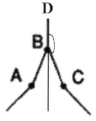

1992 Mathcounts National Sprint Round Solution

17. Solution: 216π.

As shown below in the figure, Volume of the figure generated = Volume of the cylinder − Volume of the cone

$$= \pi r^2 h - \frac{1}{3}\pi r^2 h = \frac{2}{3}\pi r^2 h = \frac{2}{3}\pi 6^2 \times 9 = 216\pi.$$

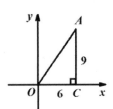
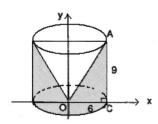

18. Solution: 3.

Add the two equations above together to get:

$7a^2 + 14ab + 7b^2 = 63$ or

$a^2 + 2ab + b^2 = 3^3 \implies (a+b)^2 = 3^2 \implies |a+b| = 3.$

19. Solution: $\dfrac{57}{16}\pi$.

Method 1:

$V_1 = \dfrac{1}{3}\pi R_1^2 h = \dfrac{1}{3}\pi \times 6^2 \times 8 = 96\pi$.

$V_2 = \dfrac{1}{3}\pi R_2^2 h_2 = \dfrac{1}{3}\pi \times R_2 \times 3 = \pi R_2$

$V_3 = \dfrac{1}{3}\pi R_3^2 h_3 = \dfrac{1}{3}\pi \times R_3 \times 2 = \dfrac{2}{3}\pi R_3$

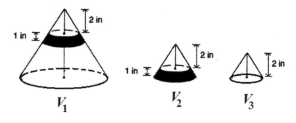

We know that $\dfrac{V_1}{V_2} = (\dfrac{h_1}{h_2})^3 = (\dfrac{8}{3})^3 = \dfrac{2^9}{3^3}$ $\implies$ $V_2 = \dfrac{3^3 \times V_1}{2^9} = \dfrac{81}{16}\pi$

$\dfrac{V_2}{V_3} = (\dfrac{h_2}{h_3})^3 = (\dfrac{3}{2})^3 = \dfrac{27}{8}$ $\implies$ $V_3 = \dfrac{8V_2}{27} = \dfrac{\frac{81}{2}\pi}{27} = \dfrac{3}{2}\pi$

$V_2 - V_3 = \dfrac{81}{16}\pi - \dfrac{3}{2}\pi = \dfrac{57}{16}\pi$.

1992 Mathcounts National Sprint Round Solution

Method 2:
Let R_1 be the radius of the base 1 (1/2 DE) and R_2 be the radius of the base 2 (1/2 FG). (see figure below).

In order to calculate the volume of the slice, we must figure out the lengths of DE and FG
Using similar triangle ratios, we have:

$\dfrac{AB}{DE} = \dfrac{HC}{IC} \Rightarrow \dfrac{12}{DE} = \dfrac{8}{3} \Rightarrow DE = \dfrac{9}{2} \Rightarrow R_1 = \dfrac{9}{4}$

$\dfrac{AB}{FG} = \dfrac{HC}{CJ} \Rightarrow \dfrac{12}{FG} = \dfrac{8}{2} \Rightarrow FG = 3 \Rightarrow R_2 = \dfrac{3}{2}$

$V = \dfrac{1}{3}\pi h(R_1^2 + R_2^2 + R_1 R_2) = \dfrac{1}{3}\pi \times 1 \times [(\dfrac{9}{4})^2 + (\dfrac{3}{2})^2 + \dfrac{9}{4} \times \dfrac{3}{2}] = \dfrac{57}{16}\pi$.

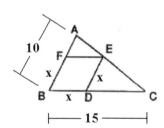

Note:
Volume of the frustum of a cone:
$V = \dfrac{1}{2}h(B_1 + B_2 + \sqrt{B_1 B_2})$, where B_1 and B_2 represent the areas of the two bases.

Volume of the frustum of a right circular cone:
$V = \dfrac{1}{3}\pi h(R_1^2 + R_2^2 + R_1 R_2)$, R_1 and R_2 represent the radius of the bases.

20. Solution: 6.
Since $\triangle ABC$ and $\triangle EDC$ are similar to each other ($DE \| AB$),
$\dfrac{10}{15} = \dfrac{x}{15-x} \rightarrow 10(15-x) = 15x$
$\rightarrow 150 - 10x = 15x \rightarrow 25x = 150 \rightarrow x = 6$.

21. Solution: – 2.
$y = \dfrac{1}{x} - 2 \Rightarrow x = \dfrac{1}{y+2} \Rightarrow f(y) = \dfrac{1}{y+2}$
$y = -2$ is not contained in the range, because the denominator cannot be 0.

22. Solution: 89.

1992 Mathcounts National Sprint Round Solution

The number of times a number occurs is one more the number of times the previous number occurs. So $1+2+3+4+\ldots+n = \dfrac{(1+n)n}{2}$ th term of the sequence is n.

$$\dfrac{(1+n)n}{2} = 4000 \quad \Rightarrow \quad (1+n)n = 8000$$

When $n = 89$, $(1+n)n = 90 \times 89 = 8010$ and $\dfrac{(1+n)n}{2} = 4005$. This means that the 4000th term is 89 (note that there are 89 "89"s and the 4000th term is the $89 - 5 = 84^{th}$ "89").

23. Solution: 12.
50! ends in $\left\lfloor \dfrac{50}{5} \right\rfloor + \left\lfloor \dfrac{50}{5^2} \right\rfloor = 10 + 2 = 12$ zeros.

24. Solution: 19.
Since no two bags may contain the same number of marbles, in order to achieve the greatest number of bags, there must be 1 marble in the first bag, 2 in the next, 3 in the next, etc.
$1+2+3+4+\ldots+n = \dfrac{(1+n)n}{2}$.
$\dfrac{(1+n)n}{2} = 190 \Rightarrow \quad n^2 + n - 380 = 0 \quad \Rightarrow n = 19$.
Note: This problem was argued be inaccurate. If one puts a bag inside another bag and repeats doing this, the greatest number of bags can be 190.

25. Solution: $\dfrac{5}{16}$.
There are 5 cases in which the two digit number de is a multiple of 3:
(4, 5); (5, 4); (5, 7); (7, 5); and (6, 6). This produces $\binom{4}{1}\binom{4}{1}$ possible two-digit numbers.

The probability that de is a multiple of 3 is $\dfrac{5}{\binom{4}{1}\binom{4}{1}} = \dfrac{5}{16}$.

26. Solution: 1.
Using the shoe-lace theorem to find the area of the triangle given the area and two of the coordinates,

1992 Mathcounts National Sprint Round Solution

$$7.5 = \frac{1}{2}\begin{vmatrix} -3 & 1 \\ -2 & -3 \\ x & 0 \\ -3 & 1 \end{vmatrix} = \frac{1}{2}(4x+11)$$

$4x + 11 = 15 \quad \Rightarrow \quad x = 1$

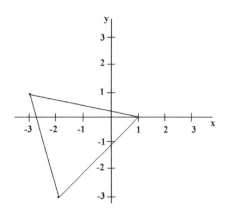

27. Solution: 24 hours.
Think of the satellites as two people, Alex and Betsy. Assume that Alex walks from A to B and Betsy walks from B to A at the same time. After t hours, they meet each other and then they continue to walk. It takes Alex t_1 hours to reach B and t_2 hours for Betsy to reach A. Assume that Alex and Betsy keep their speed constant.
The following relationship is true for $t, t_1,$ and t_2:

$$t = \sqrt{t_1 \times t_2}$$

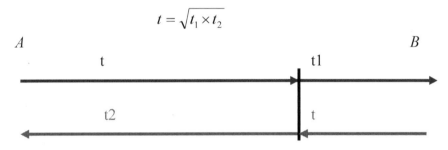

In our problem,
$t = 16$ and $t_1 = 48 - 16 = 36$.
$t^2 = t_1 \times t_2 \quad \Rightarrow \quad 16^2 = 36 \times t_2 \quad \Rightarrow \quad t_2 = 8$
The second satellite circles the earth in $8 + 16 = 24$ hours.

28. Solution: $4 + 2\sqrt{3}$.
Extend FE to meet DC at G. In $\triangle EGC$, using the Pythagorean Theorem, $EG^2 + GC^2 = EC^2 \quad \Rightarrow \quad (2x-1)^2 + x^2 = (2x)^2 \quad \Rightarrow$
$4x^2 - 4x + 1 + x^2 = 4x^2 \Rightarrow x^2 - 4x + 1 = 0$.
Solve for x using the quadratic formula to get $x_{1,2} = 2 \pm \sqrt{3}$.
Since $FE = 1$, x must be greater than 1. DC is equal to $2x = 2(2 + \sqrt{3}) = 4 + 2\sqrt{3}$.

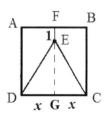

1992 Mathcounts National Sprint Round Solution

29. Solution: 16.
Since $99 = 11 \times 9$, $708,a6b,8c9$ needs to be divisible by both 9 and 11.
For the number to be divisible by 9, the sum of its digits must be divisible by 9:
$7 + 8 + a + 6 + b + 8 + c + 9 \equiv 0 \mod 9 \Rightarrow a + b + c \equiv 7 \mod 9$
This is equivalent to
$$a + b + c = 7$$
$$a + b + c = 16$$
$$a + b + c = 25.$$
For the number to be divisible by 11,
$7 + 8 + 6 + 8 + 9 - (a + b + c) \equiv 0 \mod 11.$
This is equivalent to
$$a + b + c = 5.$$
$$a + b + c = 16.$$
$$a + b + c = 27.$$

If and only if $a + b + c = 16$, will the given number be divisible by both 9 and 11.

Note: Divisibility rule for 11: To find out if a number is divisible by eleven, add every other digit, and call that sum "x." Add together the remaining digits, and call that sum "y." Take the difference, $x - y$. If the difference is zero or a multiple of eleven, then the original number is a multiple of eleven.

30. Solution: 24.
Expand 792 to get $792 = 3^2 \times 2^3 \times 11$. The number of divisors of 792 is
$(2 + 1) \times (3 + 1)(1 + 1) = 24.$

1992 Mathcounts National Target Round Solutions

1. Solution: 2.

There are $\left\lfloor \dfrac{50}{5} \right\rfloor + \left\lfloor \dfrac{50}{5^2} \right\rfloor = 10 + 2 = 12$ zeros in 50!

There are $\left\lfloor \dfrac{19}{5} \right\rfloor = 3$ zeros in 19!

There are $\left\lfloor \dfrac{31}{5} \right\rfloor + \left\lfloor \dfrac{31}{5^2} \right\rfloor = 6 + 1 = 7$ zeros in 31!

The solution is 2 (zeros): $\dfrac{10^{12}}{10^3 \times 10^7} = 10^2$.

2. Solution: 4: 5: 27.
At 4 o'clock, the angle formed by the minute hand and the hour hand is 120°. In order for the minute hand to be perpendicular to the hour hand, the minute hand needs to move an angle of 30° at the relative speed of $\dfrac{11°}{2}$ per minute in t minutes.

To find t:
$t_1 \times \dfrac{11°}{2} = 30° \quad \Rightarrow \quad t_1 = 30 \times \dfrac{2}{11} = 5 + \dfrac{5}{11}$ minutes.

5/11 minutes are 27 seconds, so the time it takes for the minute hand and the hour hands of a clock to be perpendicular to each other is 4: 5: 27.

3. Solution: 5461.
$2^{14} - 1 = (2^7 - 1)(2^7 + 1) = 127 \times 129 = 127 \times 3 \times 43$.
The largest divisor that is less $2^{14} - 1$ is $127 \times 43 = 5461$.

4. Solution: $\dfrac{4\pi}{5}$.

The area of the most outer shaded region is $\pi \times (1)^2 - \pi \times (\dfrac{1}{2})^2 = \dfrac{3\pi}{4}$.

The area of the second most outer shaded region term is $\pi \times (\dfrac{1}{4})^2 - \pi \times (\dfrac{1}{8})^2 = \dfrac{3\pi}{4^3}$.

The area of the third most outer shaded region term is $\pi \times (\dfrac{1}{16})^2 - \pi \times (\dfrac{1}{32})^2 = \dfrac{3\pi}{4^5}$.

1992 Mathcounts National Target Round Solutions

The areas form an infinite geometric sequence with the common ratio of $\dfrac{\frac{3\pi}{4}}{\frac{3\pi}{4^3}} = \dfrac{1}{4^2}$.

The sum of all the terms, or the total area, is $S = \dfrac{a_1}{1-r} = \dfrac{\frac{3\pi}{4}}{1-\frac{1}{4^2}} = \dfrac{4\pi}{5}$.

5. Solution: $\dfrac{1}{21}$.

There are $\binom{9}{4} = 126$ total ways to select four random points on the geoboard.

The number of squares is that can be formed is 6.
The probability that four randomly selected points on the geoboard will be vertices of a square is $\dfrac{6}{126} = \dfrac{1}{21}$.

6. Solution: 23.
The highest score that you cannot obtain is $9 \times 4 - (9 + 4) = 23$.

Note: The formula for problems of this type is always $m \times n - (m + n)$ if m and n are relatively prime.

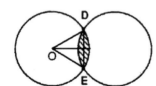

7. Solution: 7.
Triangle ODE is an equilateral triangle, as shown in the figure below.

The area of $\triangle ODE$ is $\dfrac{\sqrt{3}}{4}a^2 = \dfrac{6^2\sqrt{3}}{4} = 9\sqrt{3}$.

The area of sector ODE is $\dfrac{60\pi \times a^2}{360} = \dfrac{6^2\pi}{6} = 6\pi$.

The area of the shaded region is $2 \times (6\pi - 9\sqrt{3}) \approx 6.503 = 7$.

8. Solution: 1728.
The sum of the divisors of n is:

$$\sigma(n) = \left(\dfrac{p_1^{a+1}-1}{p_1-1}\right)\left(\dfrac{p_2^{b+1}-1}{p_2-1}\right)\ldots\left(\dfrac{p_k^{m+1}-1}{p_k-1}\right)$$

1992 Mathcounts National Target Round Solutions

or $\quad \sigma(n) = (p_1^a + p_1^{a-1} + ... + p_1^0)((p_2^b + p_2^{b-1} + ... + p_2^0)...(p_k^m + p_k^{m-1} + ... + p_k^0)$

$770 = 77 \times 10 = 7 \times 11 \times 2 \times 5$

$\sigma(770) = (7^1 + 7^0)((11^1 + 11^0)(2^1 + 2^0)(5^1 + 5^0) = 1728$.

1993 Mathcounts National Sprint Round Solutions

1. Solution: 5.
Let x be the number of people behind me. Then, the number of people ahead of me is $2 + x$ and the total number of people in line is $2 + x + 1 + x = 2x + 3$.
This equation becomes $2x + 3 = 3x \Rightarrow x = 3$
The number of people ahead of me is 5.

2. Solution: 7.
Method 1:
Since \$8 equals $\frac{1}{3}$ of the cost of the meal, the total cost of the meal is \$24.
Jim paid $24 \times \frac{5}{5+3} = 15 = 8 + 7$ dollars and John paid $24 \times \frac{3}{5+3} = 9 = 8 + 1$ dollars.
Jim paid 7 dollars more and John paid 1 dollar more. Thus 7 of Jan's 8 dollars should go to Jim and 1 dollar to John.

Method 2:
There are 8 dishes, so each person has $\frac{8}{3}$ of the dishes and must pay $\frac{8}{3}$ of the cost. Jan agreed to pay her share, 1/3 of the cost of the meal, which is 8 dollars.
Jim contributed $5 - \frac{8}{3} = \frac{7}{3}$ extra. So, he should receive x dollars of Jan's 8 dollars: $\dfrac{\frac{7}{3}}{\frac{8}{3}} = \dfrac{x}{8}$.
Solving for x, we have $x = 7$ dollars.

3. Solution: 9.
Since $125 = 5^3$, we have $a = 5$ and $b = 3$.
So $(b^a)^2 = (3^5)^2 = 3^{10} = (9)^5 = (-1)^5 \equiv 9 \pmod{10}$. The units digit is 9.

4. Solution: 4/7.
$\frac{1}{7} = 0.\overline{142857}$; $\frac{2}{7} = 0.\overline{285714}$; $\frac{3}{7} = 0.\overline{428671}$; and $\frac{4}{7} = 0.\overline{571428}$. In the fraction 4/7, the third and fourth digit form a two-digit number, 14, which is one-half of the number formed by the fifth and sixth digit, 28.

1993 Mathcounts National Sprint Round Solutions

5. Solution: 0.037.

$$\left(\frac{1}{3}\right)^3 = \frac{1}{9 \times 3} = \frac{\frac{1}{3}}{9} = \frac{0.\overline{3}}{9} \approx 0.037.$$

6. Solution: 1014.
Let the length of one edge of the cube be x. Since the volume is 2,197,
$x^3 = 2197 \Rightarrow x = 13$.
The surface area of the cube is $6x^2 = 6 \times 13^2 = 1014$.

7. Solution: 729.
We have nine digits (1 through 9) that we can use for the hundreds digit, ten's digit, and units digit. The number of 3-digit numbers that do not contain a zero is $\underline{9} \times \underline{9} \times \underline{9} = 729$.

8. Solution: $\frac{1}{38}$.

There are a total of 21 marbles in the bag. The probability of getting a red marble on the first draw is $\frac{6}{21}$. The probability of getting a red marble on the second draw is $\frac{5}{20}$. The probability of getting a blue marble in the third draw is $\frac{7}{19}$.
The probability that two red marbles and one blue marble will be drawn in that order is
$\frac{6}{21} \times \frac{5}{20} \times \frac{7}{19} = \frac{1}{38}$.

9. Solution: 4.
4 non-congruent quadrilaterals can be drawn, as shown below.

10. Solution: $\sqrt{3} - \sqrt{2}$.
Method 1:

1993 Mathcounts National Sprint Round Solutions

$$\sqrt{5-2\sqrt{3}} = \sqrt{(\sqrt{3})^2 - 2\sqrt{3}\sqrt{2} + (\sqrt{2})^2} = \sqrt{(\sqrt{3}-\sqrt{2})^2} = \sqrt{3}-\sqrt{2}.$$

Method 2:
By the formula:

$$\sqrt{a \pm \sqrt{b}} = \sqrt{\frac{a+\sqrt{a^2-b}}{2}} \pm \sqrt{\frac{a-\sqrt{a^2-b}}{2}} \text{ where } b > 0, \text{ and } a \geq \sqrt{b}.$$

$$\sqrt{5-2\sqrt{6}} = =\sqrt{5-\sqrt{24}} = \sqrt{\frac{5+\sqrt{5^2-24}}{2}} - \sqrt{\frac{5-\sqrt{5^2-24}}{2}} = \sqrt{3}-\sqrt{2}.$$

11. Solution: 15.

Since $\left(1-\frac{1}{n}\right)^{-1} = \frac{n}{n-1}$, we have $\frac{2}{2-1} \times \frac{3}{3-1} \times \frac{4}{4-1} \cdots \times \frac{15}{15-1} = \frac{2}{1} \times \frac{3}{2} \times \frac{4}{3} \cdots \times \frac{15}{14} = 15.$

12. Solution: 3.

$$f(2) = 1$$
$$f(2+2) = f(4) = \frac{2}{1}$$
$$f(4+2) = f(6) = \frac{4}{2}$$
$$f(6+2) = f(8) = \frac{6}{2} = 3$$

$f(8) = 3$.

13. Solution: $2x - 1$.

$$\frac{(1-\frac{1}{x})^{-1}+1}{(1-\frac{1}{x})^{-1}-1} = \frac{\frac{x}{x-1}+1}{\frac{x}{x-1}-1} = \frac{\frac{x+x-1}{x-1}}{\frac{x-x+1}{x-1}} = 2x-1.$$

1993 Mathcounts National Sprint Round Solutions

14. Solution: $-\dfrac{13}{3}$.

The slope of line with coordinates $(-1, 16)$ and $(2, 3)$ is equal to: $\dfrac{16-3}{-1-2} = -\dfrac{13}{3}$.

Note: Another way is to find all three slopes k_1, k_2, and k_3. If $k_1 \times k_2 = -1$, k_3 will be the slope of the line containing the hypotenuse.

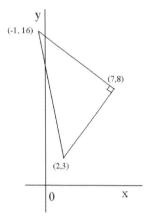

15. Solution: 11.
Method 1:
We know that the remainders will be the same when the three integers 618, 343, and 277 are divided by d. let the remainder be r.

$618 = dq_1 + r$ \hfill (1)
$343 = dq_2 + r$ \hfill (2)
$277 = dq_3 + r$ \hfill (3)
$(1) - (2): 275 = d(q_1 + q_2)$ \hfill (4)
$(2) - (3): 66 = d(q_2 + q_3)$ \hfill (5)

From (4) and (5) we know that both 275 and 66 are divisible by d.
$275 = 11 \times 25$ and $66 = 11 \times 6$. So d is 11.

Method 2:
Let the remainder be R. The following is true:
$618 \equiv R \quad \mod d$
$343 \equiv R \quad \mod d$
$277 \equiv R \quad \mod d$
$618 - 343 \equiv 0 \quad \mod d$
$343 - 277 \equiv 0 \quad \mod d$

1993 Mathcounts National Sprint Round Solutions

$275 \equiv 0 \quad \mod d$

$66 \equiv 0 \quad \mod d$

$275 = 25 \times 11$ and $66 = 6 \times 11$.

The smallest possible value of d is 11.

16. Solution: 9/16.

There are a total of $1 + 3 + 5 + 7 = 16$ small triangles. 7 of them are not shaded and $16 - 7 = 9$ of them are shaded. So the ratio of the shaded area to the total area is 9/16.

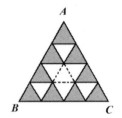

17. Solution: 18.

Let the five terms be a_1, a_2, a_3, a_4, a_5.

$a_1 + a_2 + a_3 + a_4 + a_5 = 55$ \hfill (1)

$a_3 + a_4 + a_5 = 48$ \hfill (2)

$(1) - (2)$: $a_1 + a_2 = 7$ \hfill (3)

We know that $a_3 = \dfrac{55}{5} = 11$. So the sum of the first three terms is equal to

$a_1 + a_2 + a_3 = 7 + a_3 = 7 + 11 = 18$.

Note: If $a_1 + a_2 + a_3 + a_4 + a_5 = N$, then $a_3 = \dfrac{N}{5}$

If $a_1 + a_2 + a_3 + a_4 = N$, then $\dfrac{a_2 + a_3}{2} = \dfrac{N}{4}$.

18. Solution: 47.6%.

There are 21 square numbers between 100 and 1000 ($11^2, 12^2, \ldots 31^2$). Among these squares numbers, there are 11 even square numbers ($10^2, 12^2, \ldots, 30^2$). The percent of even perfect squares is $11/21 = 47.6\%$.

19. Solution: 44100.

Note: $1^3 + 2^3 + 3^3 + \ldots + n^3 = \left(\dfrac{(1+n)n}{2}\right)^2$.

So, the sum equals $\left(\dfrac{(1+20)20}{2}\right)^2 = 44100$.

Note:

1993 Mathcounts National Sprint Round Solutions

$$1^2 + 2^2 + 3^2 + 4^2 + 5^2 + 6^2 + 7^2 + \ldots + (n-1)^2 + n^2 = \frac{n(n+1)(2n+1)}{6}$$

20. Solution: 13.

Expand: $\left(\dfrac{1}{x+y}\right)\left(\dfrac{1}{x}+\dfrac{1}{y}\right) = \left(\dfrac{1}{x+y}\right)\left(\dfrac{x+y}{xy}\right) = \dfrac{1}{xy}$.

Since $\left(\dfrac{1}{x+y}\right)\left(\dfrac{1}{x}+\dfrac{1}{y}\right) = \dfrac{1}{xy} = \dfrac{1}{13}$, the value of the product of x and y is 13.

21. Solution: 0.
There are 7 one-digit numbers and 90 two-digit numbers.
These numbers used $7 + 90 \times 2 = 187$ digits.
There are still $700 - 187 = 513$ digits remaining. There must be $513 \div 3 = 171$ three-digit numbers, so there the 171th 3-digit number starting from 100 is 270. The 700th digit is 0.

22. Solution: 13.
Method 1:
The number of digits of the exponent 2^{40} equals
$\log 2^{40} = \lceil 40 \log 2 \rceil = \lceil 40 \times 0.3010 \rceil = \lceil 12.04 \rceil = 13$.
Note: $\log 2 \approx 0.3010$ and $\log 3 \approx 0.4771$.

Method 2:
$2^{10} = 1024$
$2^{40} = (2^{10})^4 = (1024)^4 \approx = (1000)^4 = 10^{12}$. We see 12 zeros. So we can get 13 digits.

23. Solution: $\dfrac{99}{100}$.

$\dfrac{1}{2} + \dfrac{1}{6} + \dfrac{1}{12} + \ldots + \dfrac{1}{9900} = \dfrac{1}{1 \times 2} + \dfrac{1}{2 \times 3} + \dfrac{1}{3 \times 4} + \ldots + \dfrac{1}{99 \times 100}$

$= \dfrac{1}{1} - \dfrac{1}{2} + \dfrac{1}{2} = \dfrac{1}{3} + \dfrac{1}{3} - \dfrac{1}{4} + \ldots + \dfrac{1}{99} - \dfrac{1}{100} = \dfrac{1}{1} - \dfrac{1}{100} = \dfrac{99}{100}$

Note: $\dfrac{1}{n(n+1)} = \dfrac{1}{n} - \dfrac{1}{n+1}$.

1993 Mathcounts National Sprint Round Solutions

24. Solution: 48.
Using the table below, we can find our answer by reading through the problem backwards.

	Steps	A	B
	Final	64	64
Pour from B to A	c	64 + 64/2 = 96	64/2 = 32
Pour from A to B	b	96 - 96/2 = 48	32 + 48 = 80
Pour from B to A	a	48 + 40 = 88	80 - 40 = 40

Bottle A contained $88 - 40 = 48$ more ounces in the beginning.

25. Solution: 2.
The problem generates the following ratios:
$$\frac{74}{74 \times 74} = \frac{1}{74} \frac{\text{dozen eggs}}{\text{hens}} ; \quad \frac{37}{37 \times 37} = \frac{1}{37} \frac{\text{kg wheat}}{\text{hens}}$$

$$\frac{\frac{1}{37} \frac{\text{kg wheat}}{\text{hens}}}{\frac{1}{74} \frac{\text{dozen eggs}}{\text{hens}}} = 2 \frac{\text{kg wheat}}{\text{dozen eggs}}.$$ 2 kilograms of wheat are needed to produce 1 dozen eggs.

26. Solution: 45.
Let the number on the first mile marker be $\overline{AB}$. Then, the second marker with the digits in reversed order is $\overline{BA}$, and the third one is either $\overline{A0B}$ or $\overline{B0A}$.
In the first hour, Alice travels at a distance of $\overline{BA} - \overline{AB} = 10B + A - 10A - B = 9B - 9A$.
In the second hour, she travels at a distance of $\overline{B0A} - \overline{BA} = 100B + A - 10B - A = 90B$ or $\overline{A0B} - \overline{BA} = 100A + B - 10B - A = 99A - 9B$.
Since she drives at a constant speed, she covers the same distance in the second hour as she did in the first hour, so $9B - 9A = 90B$
or $9B - 9A = 99A - 9B$.
The first equation has no solutions and the second equation gives us $B = 6A$.
So $A = 1$ and $B = 6$. The rate of her car is $61 - 16 = 45$ miles per hour.

1993 Mathcounts National Sprint Round Solutions

27. Solution: 150.

Using the figure below and reading the problem backwards, we can get our answer. At the end, each player has the score of 80. Let the players be *A*, *B*, and *C*. A different player wins each of the final three rounds. In the third round, let player *A* win. In the second round, let player *B* win. In the first round, let player *C* win.

		A	B	C
A wins	End of 4th round	80	80	80
B wins	End of 3 rd round	$80 \div 2 = 40$	$80 + 40 = 120$	$80 + 40 = 120$
C wins	End of 2 nd round	$40 + 60 = 100$	$120 \div 2 = 60$	$120 + 60 = 180$
	End of 1st round	$100 + 90 = 190$	$60 + 90 = 150$	$180 \div 2 = 90$

The highest score at the end of round 1 was 150.

28. Solution: 10

There are at most 15 men who are not married, 30 who do not have a telephone, 25 who do not own a car, and 20 who do not own his own home.

In total, there are at most $15 + 30 + 25 + 20 = 90$ men who do not have at least one of the above criteria.

The smallest possible number of men who have all four is $100 - 90 = 10$.

29. Solution: 6.

Method 1:

The number	The remainder
5^1	5
5^2	4
5^3	6
5^4	2
5^5	3
5^6	1
5^7	5

So we see the pattern that the remainder repeats every power of 6.

$999,999 = 166666 \times 6 + 3$.

Thus the remainder of 5^{999999} is the same as 5^3, which is 6.

1993 Mathcounts National Sprint Round Solutions

Method 2:
We are looking for R such that
$5^{999999} \equiv R \mod 7$.
According to Fermat's Little Theorem (see below) and the fact that
$999999 \equiv 3 \mod (6)$,
$5^{999999} \equiv 5^3 \equiv 6 \mod 7$
The remainder R is 6.
Note: Fermat's little theorem: Given a prime p and a not divisible by p, then $a^{p-1} \equiv 1 \pmod{p}$.

30. Solution: 62.
We draw a chart and read the problem backwards.

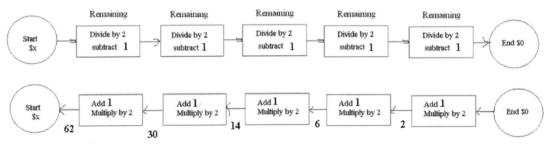

Auggie had 62 dollars when he entered the store.

1993 Mathcounts National Competition Target Round Solutions

1. Solution: 3.375.
Label the figure as follows:

$\triangle ABH \sim \triangle DEH \quad \Rightarrow \quad \dfrac{AB}{ED} = \dfrac{AH}{DH} \quad \Rightarrow \quad \dfrac{3}{1} = \dfrac{AH}{3-AH}$

$\Rightarrow \quad \dfrac{1}{3} = \dfrac{3-AH}{AH} = \dfrac{3}{AH} - 1 \quad \Rightarrow \quad AH = \dfrac{9}{4}.$

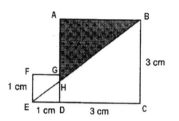

The area of the shaded region is

$\dfrac{AB \times AH}{2} = \dfrac{3 \times \dfrac{9}{4}}{2} = \dfrac{27}{8} = 3.375.$

2. Solution: $\dfrac{11}{36}$.

C is the concentration or strength of the solution; V is the volume of the solution; and S is the substance or the amount of the solution contains. The following relationship is true: $C \times V = S$.

In our problem, we have

	C	V	S
Mixture A	8/(16+8) = 1/3	24	24/3
Mixture took away	8/(16+8) = 1/3	-2	-2/3
Mixture left	8/(16+8) = 1/3	22	22/3

	C	V	S
Mixture left	8/(16+8) = 1/3	22	22/3
Water added	0	2	0
Final Mixture	x	24	22/3

x represents the concentration of grape juice in the mixture.

$x \times 24 = \dfrac{22}{3} \quad \Rightarrow \quad x = \dfrac{11}{36}.$

3. Solution: 38.
Let x be the original length of the worm.

The length of the worm at the end of the nth week	nth week
$x \times \dfrac{3}{2}$	1
$x \times \dfrac{3}{2} \times \dfrac{4}{3}$	2

1993 Mathcounts National Competition Target Round Solutions

$$x \times \frac{3}{2} \times \frac{4}{3} \times \frac{5}{4} \qquad\qquad 3$$

$$\cdots \qquad\qquad \cdots$$

$$x \times \frac{3}{2} \times \frac{4}{3} \times \frac{5}{4} \times \ldots \times \frac{n+2}{n+1} \qquad\qquad n$$

To find the number of weeks it took for the worm to become 20 times as long as it was when it was first measured, solve the below equation.

$$x \times \frac{3}{2} \times \frac{4}{3} \times \frac{5}{4} \times \ldots \times \frac{n+2}{n+1} = 20x$$

$$\frac{1}{2} \times (n+2) = 20 \to n+2 = 40 \to n = 38.$$

4. Solution: $18\sqrt[3]{2}$.

The volume of a sphere is $V = \frac{4}{3}\pi r^3$. In this problem, r equals 9.

$$\frac{4}{3}\pi 9^3 \times 2 = \frac{4}{3}\pi r^3 \qquad\Rightarrow\qquad r = 9\sqrt[3]{2}$$

$$\Rightarrow \qquad \text{Diameter} = 2r = 18\sqrt[3]{2}.$$

5. Solution: $\frac{1}{91}$.

Method 1:

The total number of ways to choose four points from the graph of 16 points is $\binom{16}{4} = 1820$.

The number of squares that can be formed using the lines below is $N_1 = 3^2 + 2^2 + 1^2 = 14$.

The number of additional squares that can be formed as shown below is $N_2 = 4 + 2 = 6$:

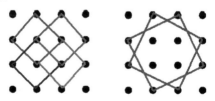

1993 Mathcounts National Competition Target Round Solutions

The probability of forming a square is $P = \dfrac{6+14}{1820} = \dfrac{1}{91}$.

Method 2:
The total number of ways to choose four points from the graph of 16 points is
$\binom{16}{4} = 1820$.

The number of squares that can be formed by the dots can be obtained by the formula:
$N = 1 \times (n-1)^2 + 2 \times (n-2)^2 + 3 \times (n-3)^2 + \ldots + (n-1) \times 1^2$ where n is the number of dots in an array. In this problem $n = 4$.
$N = 1 \times (4-1)^2 + 2 \times (4-2)^2 + 3 \times (4-3)^2 = 20$.
The probability is $P = \dfrac{20}{1820} = \dfrac{1}{91}$.

6. Solution: 14.

We begin with the right hand side of the equation: $\dfrac{181}{42} = 4 + \dfrac{13}{42}$.

We get $a = 4$ and $b + \dfrac{1}{c + \dfrac{1}{d}} = \dfrac{42}{13} = 3 + \dfrac{3}{13}$.

$b = 3$ and $c + \dfrac{1}{d} = \dfrac{13}{3} = 4 + \dfrac{1}{3}$.

So $c = 4$ and $d = 3$.
$a + b + c + d = 14$.

7. Solution: 15°.
We label the figure as follows:

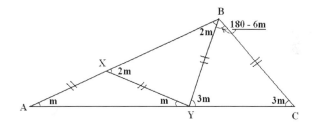

Let $\angle BAC = m$.
We are given that $\angle ABC = 120°$,
that is: $2m + 180° - 6m = 120°$
$\Rightarrow \quad m = 15°$.

8. Solution: 36481.
From statements a), b), and c), we can surmise that the smallest possible number is 16116 and the largest possible number is 81981.

1993 Mathcounts National Competition Target Round Solutions

From d) we know that the smallest possible square root is $\sqrt{16116} \approx 126 \Rightarrow 131$ (must be a palindrome) and the largest possible square root is $\sqrt{81981} \approx 286 \Rightarrow 282$ (must be a palindrome) $\Rightarrow 191$(must be a prime number).

We have the following numbers: 131, 141, 151, 161, 171, 181, and 191. However, 141 and 171 are divisible by 3 because the sum of their digits is divisible by 3, and 161 is divisible by 7 (by the divisibility rule for 7, 16 – 2 = 14), so we can narrow the list down to the following numbers: 131, 151, 181, and 191.

$131^2 = 17161$, $151^2 = 22801$, $181^2 = 32761$, $\underline{191^2 = 36481}$

The desired solution is then 36481.

1994 Mathcounts National Sprint Solution

1. Solution: z.
The value is equal to z.

$$(y \star \underbrace{(x \star w)}_{z})^{w} \star \overbrace{(y \star z)}^{x} = z \star x = z$$

2. Solution: $\dfrac{5}{16}$.

The probability is equal to $P = \dfrac{\pi \times 3^3 - \pi \times 2^2}{\pi \times 4^2} = \dfrac{5}{16}$.

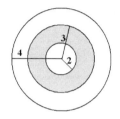

3. Solution: 128π.
The volume = Volume of the cylinder – Volume of three spheres
$$= \pi \times r^2 \times h - \dfrac{4}{3}\pi r^3 = \pi \times 4^2 \times 24 - \dfrac{4}{3}\pi 4^3 = 128\pi.$$

4. Solution: 17.
The amount of weather-stripping needed to go around the glass can be found by the sum $4 + 4 + 3.5 + 3.5 + \dfrac{2\pi \times \dfrac{3.5}{2}}{2}$. To the nearest integer, the sum is 17.

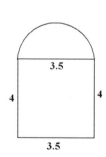

5. Solution: $80°$.
$\angle BPC = \dfrac{1}{3}(\angle ABC + \angle ACB) + \angle BAC = \dfrac{1}{3}(180° - 30°) + 30° = 80°$.

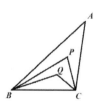

Note: There exists a following relationship between the angles shown below: $d = a + b + c$

1994 Mathcounts National Sprint Solution

6. Solution: 210.
In order to achieve the smallest possible number, a and b need to be as close as possible to each other. So, $a = 8 \times 6 \times 4 \times 1 = 192$ and $b = 7 \times 5 \times 3 \times 2 = 210$. The larger of the two numbers is 210.

7. Solution: $32.50.
A dozen roses costs $20.00, so one rose costs $\$\frac{20}{12}$.
Similarly, one daisy costs $\$\frac{5}{12}$ and one chrysanthemum costs $\$\frac{10}{12}$.
9 roses, 6 daisies, and 18 chrysanthemums will cost
$9 \times \frac{20}{12} + 6 \times \frac{5}{12} + 18 \times \frac{10}{12} = 15 + 2.5 + 15 = \$32.50$.

8. Solution: 32.
Re-write the equation as $\frac{1}{m} = \frac{2}{15} - \frac{1}{n} \to \frac{1}{m} = \frac{2n-15}{15n} \to m = \frac{15n}{2n-15}$.

m is an integer, so $2n - 15$ must be a factor of $15^2 = 3^2 5^2$, which has $(2+1)(2+1) = 9$ factors.

We can conclude that $2n - 15 < 15 \to n < 15$ from the equation $\frac{m}{n} = \frac{3 \times 5}{2n-15}$, since $m > n$ leads to $m/n > 1$ which leads to $\frac{m}{n} = \frac{3 \times 5}{2n-15} > 1$).

Since m is not a multiple of n, $2n - 15 \neq 1, 3, 5$ (otherwise $\frac{3 \times 5}{1} = 15$, $\frac{3 \times 5}{3} = 5$, $\frac{3 \times 5}{5} = 3$).
Eliminating the values that do not follow the restrictions, among the 9 factors of 15^2: 1, 3, 5, 9, 15, $3^2 \times 5$, 3×5^2, $3^2 \times 5^2$, only the factor 9 is left. So, $2n - 15 = 9 \to n = 12$, $m = 20$. $m + n = 32$.

9. Solution: 194.
Observe the sequences:
12, 14, 16, 18, ... 100.
8, 10, 12, 14, ... a

1994 Mathcounts National Sprint Solution

9, 10, 11, 12, … b
1, 2, 3, 4, … c

Let there be n terms in the arithmetic sequence from 12 to 100 with the common difference of 2.
$100 = 12 + (n-1) \times 2.$ $\Rightarrow$ $n = 45.$
a is the 45th term in the arithmetic sequence 8, 10, 12, where there is a common difference of 2.
$a = 8 + (45-1) \times 2 = 96.$
b is the 45th term in the arithmetic sequence 9, 10, 11, where there is a common difference of 1.
$b = 9 + (45-1) \times 1 = 53.$
b is the 45th term in the arithmetic sequence 1, 2, 3, where there is a common difference of 1.
$c = 1 + (45-1) \times 1 = 45.$

$a + b + c = 96 + 53 + 45 = 194.$

10. Solution: $1 + \sqrt{5}$.
Let L, W, and D be the length, width, and the diagonal of the rectangle.
$\dfrac{L}{W} = \dfrac{D}{L}$ $\Rightarrow$ $L^2 = 2D$.

According to the Pythagorean Theorem, $L^2 + W^2 = D^2 \Rightarrow L^2 = D^2 - 4$.

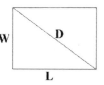

Substituting in L^2, we get
$2D = D^2 - 4 \Rightarrow D^2 - 2D - 4 = 0$.
Solve the quadratic equation to get the length of the diagonal: $D = 1 + \sqrt{5}$.

11. Solution: 4.
The reciprocal of x is $1/x$. $x - \dfrac{1}{x} = \dfrac{x^2-1}{x} = \dfrac{4x}{x} = 4.$

12. Solution: $3\dfrac{1}{2}$
$2x - 6 \leq 6$ $\Rightarrow$ $x \leq 6$
$4x + 3 \geq 13$ $\Rightarrow$ $x \geq \dfrac{5}{2}$

1994 Mathcounts National Sprint Solution

The difference between the largest and the smallest values of x is $6 - \frac{5}{2} = 3\frac{1}{2}$.

13. Solution: 19.
The smallest sum of a, b, and c is $3 + 5 + 7 = 15$.

The largest sum is $15 + 17 + 19 = 51$.
Since a, b, and c are distinct odd integers, the sum of them must be an odd integer.

By examining, $a + b + c$ can express all the odd integers from 15 to 51. There are n such numbers.

$51 = 15 + (n-1) \times 2 \Rightarrow n = 19$.

The number of odd integers between 15 and 51 is 19.

14. Solution: 0.
$3 + [2 + (1+x^2)^2]^2 = 12 \Rightarrow [2 + (1+x^2)^2]^2 = 9 \Rightarrow 2 + (1+x^2)^2 = 3$
$\Rightarrow (1+x^2)^2 = 1 \Rightarrow 1 + x^2 = 1 \Rightarrow x = 0$
$x = 0$ satisfies the equation.

15. Solution: 4.
We need to solve the following system of equations:
$$x^2 - y^2 = 12 \quad (1)$$
$$2xy = 16 \quad (2)$$
$$x^2 + y^2 = 20 \quad (3)$$
Add (3) + (2): $(x+y)^2 = 36 \Rightarrow x + y = 6 \quad (4)$
Substitute $x + y = 6$ into (1) to get $6(x - y) = 12 \Rightarrow x - y = 2 \quad (5)$
Add (4) with (5) to get $2x = 8$, $x = 4$.

16. Solution: $8 - \frac{\pi}{12}$.
The remaining volume equals the volume of the hemisphere subtracted from the volume of the cube:

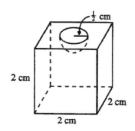

52

1994 Mathcounts National Sprint Solution

$$2^3 - \frac{\frac{4}{3}\pi(\frac{1}{2})^3}{2} = 8 - \frac{\pi}{12}.$$

17. Solution: $x = 0$ and $x = -1/3$.

The equation can become $\sqrt{y} = y$ where $y = 3x + 1$.

We can immediately see that $y = 0$ and $y = 1$ are two solutions to the equation. Then, $x = 0$ and $x = -1/3$.

18. Solution: 65.

The first four terms of the sequence are 2, 3, 5, and 9. The fifth term is $t_5 = 2 \times 9 - 1 = 17$; the sixth term is $t_6 = 2 \times 17 - 1 = 33$; the seventh term is $t_7 = 2 \times 33 - 1 = 65$.

19. Solution: 2.

The shape of the equation is the same as $|x| + |y| = 1$, except the origin is at $(-2, 3)$. The length of its diagonal is 2.

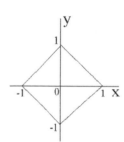

20. Solution: –4.

Complete the square: $y = x^2 - 6x + 5 = x^2 - 6x + 9 - 4 = (x-3)^2 - 4$. The minimum value of the function is –4.

21. Solution: 8.

$$\frac{7!\,8!\,9!}{7!+8!+9!} = \frac{8!\,N!}{9} \Rightarrow \frac{7!\,\cancel{8!}\,9!}{7!+8!+9!} = \frac{\cancel{8!}\,N!}{9} \Rightarrow \frac{7!\,9!}{7!+8!+9!} = \frac{N!}{9}$$

$$\frac{7!\,9!}{7!(1+8+9\times 8)} = \frac{N!}{9} \Rightarrow \frac{\cancel{7!}\,9!}{\cancel{7!}\times 9^2} = \frac{N!}{\cancel{9}} \Rightarrow \frac{9!}{9} = \frac{N!}{1} \Rightarrow 9! = 9 \times N!$$

$$\Rightarrow 9 \times 8! = 9 \times N! \Rightarrow 8! = N! \Rightarrow N = 8.$$

1994 Mathcounts National Sprint Solution

22. Solution: 6.
We know that N is the number of sides of the polygon. The number of diagonals is $\binom{N}{2} - N$.

According to the problem, $N = 2\sqrt{\binom{N}{2} - N}$ (1)

Square both sides of (1):
$N^2 = 4\binom{N}{2} - 4N \Rightarrow N^2 = 4 \times \frac{N(N-1)}{2} - 4N \Rightarrow N^2 = 2N^2 - 6N \Rightarrow$
$N = 6.$

23. Solution: 1.7:1.
Let the side length of the small square be x. The side length of the larger square follows as $x\sqrt{3}$. The ratio of the perimeters is equal to $\frac{4x\sqrt{3}}{4x} = \sqrt{3}:1$. Rounded to the nearest tenth, this ratio is 1.7:1.

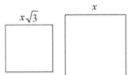

24. Solution: $\frac{NX}{M}$.

M people paid a total of $\$X$, so each person paid $\frac{X}{M}$. Since each person pays the same fare if there are an additional N people, the total money to travel becomes $(M+N) \times \frac{X}{M}$.

$(M+N) \times \frac{X}{M} - M \times \frac{X}{M} = \frac{NX}{M}.$

25. Solution: 150.
Let a, b, and c be the three side lengths of the right triangle.
According to the problem, we have
$a + b + c = 60$ (1)
$a^2 + b^2 = c^2$ (2)
$\frac{a \times b}{2} = \frac{12 \times c}{2} \rightarrow ab = 12c$ (3)

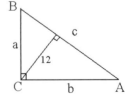

1994 Mathcounts National Sprint Solution

Square both sides of (1) to get $a^2 + b^2 + c^2 + 2ab + 2bc + 2ac = 60^2$.
Substituting (2) and (3) into the above equation, we can obtain
$2c^2 + 2 \times 12c + 2cb + 2ca = 60^2$
$\Rightarrow 2c^2 + 2 \times 12c + 2c(b+a) = 60^2$
$\Rightarrow 2c^2 + 2 \times 12c + 2c(60-c) = 60^2$
$\Rightarrow 144c = 60^2$
$\Rightarrow 6c = 150$

The area of the triangle equals $\dfrac{12 \times c}{2} = 6c = 150$.

26. Solution: $5.
Every month, Mr. Smith loses 11.50 dollars by withdrawing $10 and paying a service charge of $1.50. In eight months, he will lose $11.50 \times 8 = 92$ dollars. His balance will be 97.00 – 92.00 = $5.

27. Solution: 3.6%.
There are $4(m-2) + 4(n-2) + 4(r-2) = 208$ cubes with two-sides painted (see table below). The percent of the block made up with cubes with exactly two sides painted red is equal to $\dfrac{208}{30 \times 16 \times 12} = 3.6\%$.

Note: Below is a nifty table describing how many cubes are painted how many faces.

Cube dimension	3×3×3	4×4×4	5×5×5	n×n×n	m×n×r
3 sides painted	8	8	8	8	8
2 sides painted	12	24	36	$(n-2)^1 \times 2 \times 6$	$4(m-2) + 4(n-2) + 4(r-2)$
1 sides painted	6	24	54	$(n-2)^2 \times 1 \times 6$	$2(m-2)(n-2) + 2(m-2)(r-2) + 2(n-2)(r-2)$
0 sides painted	1	8	27	$(n-2)^3$	$(m-2)(n-2)(r-2)$
Total number of cubes	27	64	125	n^3	m×n×r

1994 Mathcounts National Sprint Solution

28. Solution: 1920.

The number of one-inch square tiles in 120 eight-inch square tiles is $120 \times 8 \times 8$. The number of one-inch square tiles in a two-inch square tile is $2 \times 8 \times 8$. $\dfrac{120 \times 8 \times 8}{2 \times 2} = 1920$ two-inch tiles must be bought to cover 120 eight-inch tiles.

29. Solution: 620.
$9^{2x+2} = (3^{x+1})^4 = 5^4 = 625$.

30. Solution: $6800.
Let x represent the purchase price of the house.
$x \times (1 + \dfrac{8.5}{100}) = 73780 \qquad \Rightarrow \qquad x = \$6800$.

1994 Mathcounts National Target Solution

1. Solution: 6.
Method 1:
$\underline{123456789101112} = 7m + 5$, where m is a positive integer.

$\underline{123456789101112\ d} = \underline{123456789101112} \times 10 + d = (7m + 5) \times 10 + d = 70m + 50 + d$
$= 70m + 7 \times 7 + 1 + d$.
Since $\underline{123456789101112\ d}$ is divisible by 7, $1 + d$ must be divisible by 7. So $d = 6$.

Method 2:
We are asked to find digit d such that:
$\underline{123456789101112\ d} = \underline{123456789101112} \times 10 + d \equiv 0 \mod 7$
Since $n - 2d$ is divisible by 7, we know that:
$\underline{123456789101112} - 2d \equiv 0 \mod 7$ \hfill (1)
We are also given that: $\underline{123456789101112} \equiv 5 \mod 7$.
So (1) becomes: $5 - 2d \equiv 0 \mod 7 \Rightarrow 7 + 5 - 2d \equiv 0 \mod 7 \Rightarrow 12 - 2d \equiv 0 \mod 7$.
So $d = 12/2 = 6$.

2. Solution: 12.
Let x be the total number of teachers and y be each person's share.
We have
$xy = 78$.
$(x - 2)(y + 1.3) = 78$

$\to xy + 1.3x - 2y - 2.6 = xy \to 1.3x - 2y = 2.6 \to 13x - 2 \times \dfrac{780}{x} = 26$

$\to x - 2 \times \dfrac{60}{x} = 2 \to x^2 - 2x - 120 = 0 \to (x + 10)(x - 12) = 0$
$x = 12$ teachers.

3. Solution: $\dfrac{1}{9}$.

$\{0!, (\dfrac{1}{2})^{-1}, \sqrt[3]{-1}\} = \{1, 2, -1)\}$ and $\{\dfrac{6!}{5!}, -\sqrt{\dfrac{1}{4}}, -1\} = \{6, -\dfrac{1}{2}, -1)\}$

For two lines to be parallel, their slopes must be equivalent. Thus, the slope for l_1 is -1 and the slope for l_2 is also -1.

The probability that l_1 and l_2 are parallel is then $P = \dfrac{1}{3} \times \dfrac{1}{3} = \dfrac{1}{9}$.

1994 Mathcounts National Target Solution

4. Solution: 12.
We see that k, n, and m are positive integers and none of them is smaller than 1. Since we want to obtain the smallest value of $k + n + m$, so we let $k = 2$.

$$\frac{19}{20} < \frac{1}{2} + \frac{1}{n} + \frac{1}{m} < 1 \Rightarrow \frac{19}{20} - \frac{1}{2} < \frac{1}{n} + \frac{1}{m} < 1 - \frac{1}{2} \Rightarrow \frac{9}{20} < \frac{1}{n} + \frac{1}{m} < \frac{1}{2}.$$

We know that $\frac{1}{n} < \frac{1}{2}$ so $n > 2$.

Again since we want to get the smallest value of $k + n + m$, we let $n = 3$.

$$\frac{9}{20} < \frac{1}{3} + \frac{1}{m} < \frac{1}{2} \Rightarrow \frac{9}{20} - \frac{1}{3} < \frac{1}{m} < \frac{1}{2} - \frac{1}{3} \Rightarrow \frac{7}{60} < \frac{1}{m} < \frac{1}{6} \Rightarrow \frac{60}{7} < m < 6$$

m is an integer so $m = 7$ or 8.

Both values work:
$$\frac{19}{20} < \frac{1}{2} + \frac{1}{3} + \frac{1}{7} = \frac{41}{42} < 1 \qquad \frac{19}{20} < \frac{1}{2} + \frac{1}{3} + \frac{1}{8} = \frac{23}{24} < 1$$

So the smallest value of $k + n + m$ is $2 + 3 + 7 = 12$.

5. Solution: 2.2.
The expression is equivalent to
$$1 + \frac{1}{2} + \frac{1}{3} + \frac{1}{4} + \frac{1}{5} + (\frac{1}{6} - \frac{1}{6}) + (\frac{1}{7} - \frac{1}{7}) + ... + (\frac{1}{95} - \frac{1}{95}) - \frac{1}{96} - \frac{1}{97} - \frac{1}{98} - \frac{1}{99} - \frac{1}{100}$$
$$= 1 + \frac{1}{2} + \frac{1}{3} + \frac{1}{4} + \frac{1}{5} - \frac{1}{96} - \frac{1}{97} - \frac{1}{98} - \frac{1}{99} - \frac{1}{100} = 2.2.$$

6. Solution: 100°.
The angle bisector of angle BAC and the exterior angle bisector of CBD meet at point E. The exterior angle of one of the angles in a triangle is equal to the sum of the two other angles in the triangle. So,
$b = a + 50° \Rightarrow 2b = 2a + 100°$ and
$\angle ACB + 2a = 2b = 2a + 100° \qquad \Rightarrow \qquad \angle C = 100°$

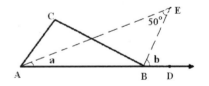

7. Solution: $27 + 2.25\pi$.
The length of the band is the circumference of one full circle and the length of $3 \times 4 = 12$ diameters.
The band's length is then

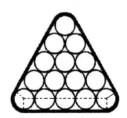

58

1994 Mathcounts National Target Solution

$12 \times 2.25 + \pi \times (\frac{2.25}{2})^2 = 27 + 2.25\,\pi$.

8. Solution: 112.5.

Let A be the maximum area the can be enclosed and x and y be the sides of the smaller rectangle as shown below.

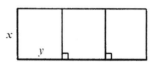

We have:
$A = x \times 3y$.

The farmer used 60 meters of fence, so
$4x + 6y = 60 \implies x = (30 - 3y)/2$.
$A = x \times 3y = 3y(\frac{30 - 3y}{2})$.
$2A = 3y(30 - 3y) = -9(y^2 - 10y) = -9(y - 5)^2 + 9 \times 5^2$

The greatest value of $2A$ is achieved by letting $y = 5$. The largest area that can be enclosed is $\frac{9 \times 5^2}{2} = 112.5$.

1995 Mathcounts National Sprint Round Solution

1. Solution: $4 + 4\sqrt{2}$.

From the Pythagorean Theorem, $AC = \sqrt{1^2 + 1^2} = \sqrt{2}$. One side of the regular octagon is equal to $\sqrt{2}$, so the length of BD equals $2 + \sqrt{2}$.

We can find the area of the octagon by subtracting the area of the four small triangles (ex. $\triangle ABC$) from the area of the square.

$(2+\sqrt{2})^2 - \dfrac{1 \times 1}{2} \times 4 = 4 + 4\sqrt{2}$.

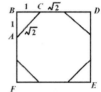

2. Solution: 0.

Let there be n zeros at the end of 20!

$n = \left\lfloor \dfrac{20}{5} \right\rfloor = 4$ (see below). There are 4 zeros at the end of 20! and there are 4 zeros for 10^4. The number of zeros in the division is $4 - 4 = 0$.

Note: N is the number of zeros n! end and $N = \left\lfloor \dfrac{n}{5^1} \right\rfloor + \left\lfloor \dfrac{n}{5^2} \right\rfloor + \left\lfloor \dfrac{n}{5^3} \right\rfloor + \left\lfloor \dfrac{n}{5^4} \right\rfloor + ...$

3. Solution: 190.

Below is a figure of the sculpture.
The surface area viewed from the front and back is equal to $(1^2 + 3^2 + 5^2) \times 2$.
The surface area viewed from the left and right is equal to $(1^2 + 3^2 + 5^2) \times 2$.

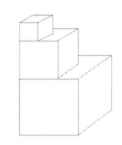

The surface area viewed from the top and bottom is equal to $5^2 \times 2$.
The total surface area, or the number of square inches of the painted surface is the sum
$(1^2 + 3^2 + 5^2) \times 2 + (1^2 + 3^2 + 5^2) \times 2 + 5^2 \times 2 = 190$.

4. Solution: 106.

If 106 students get 1 point and one student gets 0 points, the class mean will be 106/107, which is less than 1. Therefore, 106 students will be awarded extra credits. This is the largest number.

5. Solution: 40.

Let the number of boys be b and the number of girls be g.
$b + g = 75$
After a growth of 25% for girls and 40% for boys, we get

1995 Mathcounts National Sprint Round Solution

$1.4b + 1.25g = 99$
Solve this system of equations by first multiplying the first equation by 1.4 and subtracting the second equation from the result to obtain $0.15g = 6$,
$g = 40$.

6. Solution: $\dfrac{\sqrt[3]{4}}{2}$.

The volume of the sphere is equivalent to the volume of the hemisphere. Let the radius of the sphere be r_1 and the ratio of the hemisphere be r_2.

$$\frac{4}{3}\pi r_1^3 = \frac{\frac{4}{3}\pi r_2^3}{2} \quad \Rightarrow \quad \frac{r_1}{r_2} = \frac{\sqrt[3]{4}}{2}$$

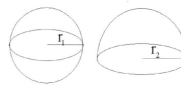

7. Solution: 27.
Let x be the number of ounces of 20% acid solution that must be mixed with a 30% acid solution.

	Concentration	Volume	Substance
A	0.2	x	$0.2 \times x$
B	0.3	$45 - x$	$0.3(45 - x)$
C	0.24	45	0.24×45

Mixture A is the 20% acid solution and mixture B is the 30% acid solution. The sum of the substance, or amount of acid, in mixtures A and C should equal to the amount of acid in the final mixture, C.
$0.2x + 0.3(45 - x) = 0.24 \times 0.45 \quad \Rightarrow \quad x = 27.$

8. Solution:
The mean is 32. So $18 + 21 + 23 + a + 36 + 37 + b = 32 \times 7 \quad \Rightarrow \quad a + b = 88$.
The median of the list is 30, so $a = 30$ and $b = 58$.
18   21   24   30   36   37   58
The positive difference between a and b is $58 - 30 = 28$.

9. Solution: $\sqrt{5}x$.
The sum of the areas of the two original equilateral triangles is equal
to $A = \dfrac{\sqrt{3}}{4}x^2 + \dfrac{\sqrt{3}}{4}(2x)^2 = \dfrac{\sqrt{3}}{4} \times 5 \times x^2 = \dfrac{\sqrt{3}}{4}(x\sqrt{5})^2$

1995 Mathcounts National Sprint Round Solution

An equilateral triangle with the same area as the sum has a length of $\sqrt{5}x$.

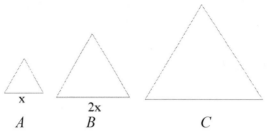

10. Solution: $\dfrac{13}{20}$.

There are a total of $\binom{6}{3}$ ways to choose three straws from the six straws. There are seven cases in which a triangle can not be formed (when the sum of two sides is less than or equal to the third side): 2, 3, 5; 2, 3, 6; 2, 3, 7; 2, 4, 6; 2, 4, 7; 3, 4, 7.

The probability that a triangle can be formed is equal to $P = 1 - \dfrac{7}{\binom{6}{3}} = 1 - \dfrac{7}{20} = \dfrac{13}{20}$.

11. Solution: 16.

The region determined by the two equations is shaded below. The area of the shaded region, or triangle, is equal to $\dfrac{1}{2} \times \dfrac{8 \times 8}{2} = 16$.

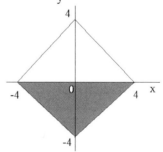

12. Solution: 2.

We can rewrite the given equation as:

$n^2 - 9n + 20 = 16 - n^2$ (1)
and $n^2 - 9n + 20 = -(16 - n^2)$ (2)

Solving (1), we get $n = 4$ or 0.5; solving (2) we get $n = 4$.
The product is $4 \times 0.5 = 2$.

1995 Mathcounts National Sprint Round Solution

13. Solution: $\dfrac{24}{25}$.

Let the length of the rectangle be x.

The perimeter is equal to $\dfrac{2}{3}x \times 2 + x + x = 4 \Rightarrow x = \dfrac{6}{5}$.

The area of the rectangle is $\dfrac{2}{3}x \times x = \dfrac{2}{3} \times \dfrac{36}{25} = \dfrac{24}{25}$.

14. Solution: 50.

The smallest three-digit odd number greater than 299 is 310 and the greatest is 999.
The number of such odd integers is n and
$999 = 301 + (n-1) \times 2 \qquad \Rightarrow \qquad n = 350$.

15. Solution: 4.

Let n be number of nickels, d be number of dimes, and q be number of quarters.
According to the problem,
$n + d + q = 30$ \hfill (1)
$5n + 10d + 25q = 500$ \hfill (2)

The question stated that q can be zero; however, if q is zero, 30 coins of dimes and nickels are not enough to make \$5. So none of n, d, or q is zero.
From multiply equation (1) by 5 and subtract the result from (2) to get:
$d + 4q = 70$ \hfill (3)

From (3) we can deduce that q must be less than 18.
If $q = 17$, then $d = 2$ (from (3)) and $n = 11$ (from (1))
If $q = 16$, then $d = 6$ and $n = 8$
If $q = 15$, then $d = 10$ and $n = 5$
If $q = 14$, then $d = 14$ and $n = 2$
If $q = 13$, then $d = 18$ and $n = -2$ (not possible).
So we can conclude that there are 4 different combinations.

16. Solution: 1.
Method 1:

The number	The remainder
9^1	2
9^2	4
9^3	1
9^4	2

1995 Mathcounts National Sprint Round Solution

So we see the pattern that the remainder repeats every power of 2.
$1995 = 285 \times 7 + 0$.
Thus the remainder of 9^{1995} is the same as 9^3, which is 1.

Method 2:
In order to solve this problem, we employ modular arithmetic. Since $\phi(7) = 7^1 - 7^0 = 6$ we can simplify 1995 into $1995 - 6 \times 332 = 3$. The exponent 9^{1995} can be reduced to 9^3. The remainder when 9 is divided by 7 is 2, so the exponent can be further reduced to 2^3. This equals 8, which when divided by 7, gives a remainder of 1.

17. Solution: 81π.
Method 1:
The shaded area is equal to $A = \pi R^2 - \pi r^2 = \pi(R^2 - r^2) = \pi \times 9^2 = 81\pi$.

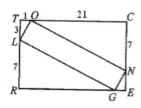

Method 2: Let the radius of the smaller circle be zero, and the shaded region becomes a circle with the radius of 9. The area of this region is $\pi r^2 = 81\pi$.

18. Solution: –2.
The rest of the sequence can be filled in as shown:
$7, a, 7 + a, 7 + 2a, 14 + 3a$.

So $14 + 3a = 11$, and $a = -2$.

19. Solution: 70.
$\triangle TLO \sim \triangle CON$ ($\angle TLO + \angle TOL = 90°$; $\angle TOL + \angle CON = 90°$, so $\angle TLO = \angle CON$; $\angle TOL = \angle CNO$).
$\dfrac{1}{7} = \dfrac{3}{OC} \Rightarrow OC = 21$.

The area of *LONG* can be found by subtracting the area of triangles *OCN*, *NEG*, *LRG*, and *TLO* from the area of the large rectangle *RECT*:
$(21+1) \times (3+7) - \dfrac{3 \times 1}{2} \times 2 - \dfrac{21 \times 7}{2} \times 2 = 220 - 150 = 70$.

64

1995 Mathcounts National Sprint Round Solution

20. Solution: $\dfrac{3^9}{2^{18}}$

Observe the following pattern:

  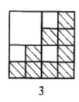

Figure 1   Figure 2   Figure 3   Figure 4   …   Figure 10

$\dfrac{3^0}{4^0}$ $\dfrac{3^1}{4^1}$ $\dfrac{3^2}{4^2}$ $\dfrac{3^3}{4^4}$ … $\dfrac{3^9}{4^9}$

The fractional part of the tenth figure that is shaded will be $\dfrac{3^9}{2^{18}}$.

21. Solution: 20.
Using the function's definition, we can get the following values.
$f(1) = f(0) + 2 = 0 + 2 \times 1 = 2$ $f(2) = f(1) + 2 \times 2 = 2 + 4 = 6$
$f(3) = f(2) + 2 \times 3 = 6 + 6 = 12$ $f(4) = f(3) + 2 \times 4 = 12 + 8 = 20$.

22. Solution: 24 cm.
Let the side length of the rectangle be a and width be b. The perimeter equals $2(a + b) = 20 \Rightarrow a + b = 15$. Since the same number of tiles can also be used to form a square region, $a \times b$ must be a square number. It is easy to see that $a = 12$ and $b = 3$.
So the square has the area 36 and side length of 6 and perimeter of $4 \times 6 = 24$ cm.

23. Solution: 144.
Draw four line segments as show in the figure below. The total area of the cross-section is equal to the subtraction of the areas of two semicircles from the addition of the areas of two semicircles and area of the 12 by 12 square. This equals $12 \times 12 = 144$.

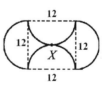

24. Solution: 6.
$3 = f(0) = a 2^{b \times 0}$ $\Rightarrow$ $a = 3$.
$24 = f(1) = 3 \times 2^{b \times 1}$ $\Rightarrow$ $2^b = 8$ $\Rightarrow$ $b = 3$

1995 Mathcounts National Sprint Round Solution

The sum of a and b is equal to $a + b = 3 + 3 = 6$.

25. Solution: 8.
We have three cases.

Case I:
If we have zero switches on, we have one way to arrange the four switches:
Off Off Off Off

Case II:
If we have one switch on and the other three off, there are $\frac{4!}{3!} = 4$ arrangements:

On   Off Off Off
Off On   Off Off
Off Off On   Off
Off Off Off On

Case III: If we have two switches on and two off so that no two adjacent switches are on, there are $\frac{4!}{2!2!} - 3 = 3$ arrangements:

On   Off On   Off
On   Off Off On
Off On   Off On

There are a total of $1 + 4 + 3 = 8$ arrangements.

26. Solution: 65.
Using the given relationship, we can say
$$\frac{c \text{ chirps}}{15 \text{ seconds}} = \frac{500 \text{ chirps}}{5 \times 60 \text{ seconds}} \Rightarrow c = 25$$
$$c = t - 40 \Rightarrow t = c + 40 = 25 + 40 = 65.$$

27. Solution: 50.
The mean speed is equal to the total distance traveled divided by the total time traveled. The total distance covered was 260×2. Using the distance-speed formula, the total time traveled for the round trip was $\frac{260}{65} + \frac{260}{40}$.

1995 Mathcounts National Sprint Round Solution

The mean speed is equal to the total distance traveled divided by the total time traveled, which is $V = \dfrac{2}{\dfrac{1}{65} + \dfrac{1}{40}} \approx 50$.

28. Solution: 36.
If a number is divisible by 4, its last two digits must form a number divisible by 4. We have the following six cases:

$$\underline{}\,\underline{}\,5\,2 \qquad \underline{}\,\underline{}\,7\,2$$

$$\underline{}\,\underline{}\,2\,4 \qquad \underline{}\,\underline{}\,6\,4$$

$$\underline{}\,\underline{}\,5\,6 \qquad \underline{}\,\underline{}\,7\,6$$

We have $3 \times 2 = 6$ ways to fill the two empty spaces in each 4-digit number so that the digits do not repeat. So, there are a total of $6 \times 6 = 36$ numbers

29. Solution: 4.
Observe the triangle below. Only in row 2^n does the entire row consist of even numbers (except for the ends). Out of the first 20 rows, 4 rows have the property.

```
Row 0                         1
1                          1     1                   2¹
2                       1    2    1
3                    1    3    3    1
4                 1    4    6    4    1              2²
5              1    5   10   10   5    1
6           1    6   15   20   15   6    1
7        1    7   21   35   35   21   7    1
8     1    8   28   56   70   56   28   8    1      2³
..    ---------------------------------------
16                                                    2⁴
..    ---------------------------------------
32                                                    2⁵
```

30. Solution: $\dfrac{n-1}{n+2}$.

$$\dfrac{k(n-2)!}{(n+1)!} = \dfrac{(n-1)(n-2)!}{(n+2)(n+1)!} \quad \Rightarrow \quad k = \dfrac{n-1}{n+2}.$$

1995 Mathcounts National Target Round Solution

1. Solution: 13.
The area of the region above equals the area of a rectangle and a trapezoid, or $3 \times 3 + \frac{(1+3)2}{2} = 9 + 4 = 13$ square units.

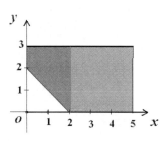

2. Solution: 83.
The formula to finding the largest finite score that cannot be attained is equal to
$N = m \times n - (m + n) = 7 \times 15 - (7 + 15) = 83$.

3. Solution: 347.
The first row contains 1 number, the second row contains 3 numbers, the third row contains 5 numbers, and so on.
The sum of n odd numbers starting from 1 equals n^2 or
$1 + 3 + 5 + 7 + \ldots + (2n - 1) = n^2 \Rightarrow 3 + 5 + 7 + \ldots + (2n - 1) = n^2 - 1$.
Let 12,000 be in the nth row.
$n^2 - 1 \leq 120{,}000 \leq n^2 \Rightarrow n = 347$.
12,000 is in the 347th row.

4. Solution: 12.11.
The perimeter of the polygon using the Pythagorean Theorem is equal to
$4 \times \sqrt{2^2 + 1^2} + \sqrt{3^2 + 1^2} = 4\sqrt{5} + \sqrt{10} = 12.11$

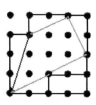

5. Solution: 47.
First we count the number of rectangles in the big square (figure a).
There are 4 possible lengths and 4 possible width for the rectangle. Since every rectangle has 2 lengths and 2 widths, there are $\binom{4}{2} \times \binom{4}{2} = 36$ such rectangles.

Next, we count the number of rectangles in the smaller square (figure b).

1995 Mathcounts National Target Round Solution

There are $\binom{3}{2} \times \binom{3}{2} = 9$ such squares.

Finally, we count the last two rectangles (figure c).

The total number of rectangles in the diagram is $36 + 9 + 2 = 47$.

Figure a Figure b Figure c

6. Solution: 1.
We calculate $f(5)$ first: $f(5) = 5 - f(f(8)) = 5 - f(6) = 5 - 4 = 1$.

$f(4) = 4 - f(f(7)) = 4 - f(5) = 4 - 1 = 3$ and
$f(3) = 3 - f(f(6)) = 3 - f(4) = 3 - 3 = 0$.

Using our values for f(4) and f(3), we can figure out f(1):
$f(1) = 1 - f(f(4)) = 1 - f(3) = 1 - 0 = 1$.

7. Solution: 2300.
The circumference of the corral can be calculated as: $20 \times (8 + \frac{1}{2}) = 170$ feet.

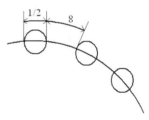

The radius of the corral is then $r = \dfrac{170}{\pi}$.

The area of the corral is $\pi r^2 = \pi(\dfrac{170}{\pi})^2 = 2299.29 \approx 2300$.

8. Solution: (0, 1).
The equation of the line connecting A and its reflection point A^1 has the slope $-1/2$ and passes through the point $(-2, 2)$. The equation of this line is $y = -\dfrac{1}{2}x + 1$.

The point of intersection of the lines $y = -\dfrac{1}{2}x + 1$ and $y = 2x + 1$ is

$-\dfrac{1}{2}x + 1 = 2x + 1 \rightarrow x = 0, y = 1 \rightarrow (0, 1)$.

1995 Mathcounts National Target Round Solution

Let the coordinate of A^1 be denoted as (a, b). By the midpoint formula, we have:
$$\frac{a-2}{2} = 0 \implies a = 2.$$
$$\frac{b-(-2)}{2} = 1 \implies b = 0.$$
The coordinates of the reflection of A is $(2, 0)$.

1996 Mathcounts National Sprint Round Solution

1. Solution: 5400.
Let the three integers be $2x$, $2x + 1$, and $2x + 3$. The sum is equal to
$2x + 2x + 1 + 2x + 3 = 220 \rightarrow 6x + 4 = 220 \rightarrow 6x = 216 \rightarrow x = 36$.
The product of three numbers is equal to $72 \times 73 \times 75 = 5400$.

2. Solution: 115.
According to the problem,
$$O + S = 110 \quad (1)$$
$$C + S = 103 \quad (2)$$
$$C + P = 108 \quad (3)$$
We would like to calculate the sum of the weights of Oinker and Porker, or $O+P$.
The difference between equations 1 and 2 is
(1) – (2): $\quad O - C = 7 \quad (4)$
(4 + (3)): $\quad O + P = 115$
Oinker and Porker weighed 115 pounds together.

3. Solution: 4π.
Since $\angle RIP = 36°$ and O is the center of the circle, $\angle ROP = 2 \times 36 = 72°$.
The circumference of the circle, $2\pi r$, is essentially an arc of 360 degrees. So, an arc of 72 degrees measures x, where $\dfrac{360°}{2\pi r} = \dfrac{72°}{x}$.
$r = 10$, so $x = 4\pi$.

4. Solution: 3.
Multiply the inequalities by 72 to get $36 \leq 9x \leq 56$. x can be 4, 5, or 6. There are 3 integral solutions.

5. Solution: 0.504.
There are a total of $9 \times 10 \times 10 \times 10$ four-digit numbers and $9 \times 9 \times 8 \times 7$ four-digit numbers where no two of its digits are the same. The probability is equal to
$$\dfrac{9 \times 9 \times 8 \times 7}{9 \times 10 \times 10 \times 10} = 0.504.$$

1996 Mathcounts National Sprint Round Solution

6. Solution: 0.39.
If point *E* is chosen inside the semicircle, triangle *ABE* will always be obtuse. We are then looking for the ratio of the area of the shaded region in the figure below (a semicircle) to the area of the square.

The answer will be $P = \dfrac{\frac{1}{2}\pi\left(\frac{1}{2}AB\right)^2}{AB^2} = \dfrac{\pi}{8} = 0.39$.

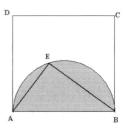

7. Solution: 2.
Raise the entire expression to the nth power to obtain $3^n < 100 < 5^n$
Only when $n = 3$ or 4 is this inequality true, so there are 2 values of *n*.

8. Solution: 12.
101, 808, 111, 888, 181, 818, 609, 619, 689, 906, 916, and 986.

9. Solution: 46.
The following rectangles have areas no more than 25 square units:

$1 \times 1, 1 \times 2, \ldots 1 \times 25$	25 triangles
$2 \times 2, 2 \times 3, \ldots 2 \times 12$	11 triangles
$3 \times 3, 3 \times 4, \ldots 3 \times 8$	6 triangles
$4 \times 4, 4 \times 5, 4 \times 6$	3 triangles
5×5	1 triangle

There are a total $25 + 11 + 6 + 3 + 1 = 46$ such triangles.

10. Solution: 50.
Ranking the numbers from least to greatest, we know that the median, middle number, is 19. In order to achieve the greatest possible range, let the first number be 0 and the second number be 1 and the second to last numbers be 1 and 20, respectively. The remaining, greatest number will be $18 \times 5 - 19 - 1 - 20 = 50$. The list of the five numbers can be 0, 1, 19, 20, 50. The greatest range is 50.

11. Solution: 96.
There are $4 \times 3 \times 3 + 2 \times 2 \times 7 = 64$ cubes in total. To get smallest surface area of the re-arrangement, we need to arrange the length of the three dimensions to be close as

1996 Mathcounts National Sprint Round Solution

possible to each other. In this case, it will be a 4 × 4 × 4 solid. The surface area of this cube is 4 × 4 × 6 = 96.

12. Solution: 9.
Method 1:
The quadrilateral is shown in the figure below. Its area is equal to the subtraction of the two adjacent right triangles to the area of the surrounding rectangle: $4 \times 3 - \dfrac{3 \times 1}{2} - \dfrac{3 \times 1}{2} = 9$.

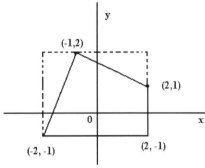

Method 2:
For a quadrilateral, given vertices in the order clockwise (x_1, y_1), (x_2, y_2), (x_3, y_3), and (x_4, y_4), the area is

$$A = \dfrac{1}{2} \begin{vmatrix} x_1 & y_1 \\ x_2 & y_2 \\ x_3 & y_3 \\ x_4 & y_4 \\ x_1 & y_1 \end{vmatrix} = \dfrac{1}{2}((x_1 y_2 + x_2 y_3 + x_3 y_4 + x_4 y_1) - (x_1 y_4 + x_4 y_3 + x_3 y_2 + x_2 y_1))$$

Or $A = \dfrac{1}{2} \begin{vmatrix} -1 & 2 \\ 2 & 1 \\ 2 & -1 \\ -2 & -1 \\ -1 & 2 \end{vmatrix} = \dfrac{1}{2} \times |-18| = 9$.

13. Solution: $\dfrac{4}{49}$.

$15^{90} = 15^{65} \times (15^{25}) = 15^{65} \times ((3^{25}) \times (5^{25}))$

There are $(25 + 1)(25 + 1)$ factors that are multiples of 15^{65}.
There are $(90 + 1)(90 + 1)$ factors that are multiples of 15^{90}.
The probability that a random factor of 15^{90} is a multiple of 15^{65} is $\dfrac{26 \times 26}{91 \times 91} = \dfrac{4}{49}$.

1996 Mathcounts National Sprint Round Solution

14. Solution: 60.
The perimeter of this triangle is equal to 36. From the Pythagorean Theorem,

$\begin{array}{l} x^2 - y^2 = 12^2 \\ 2x + 2y = 36 \end{array} \Rightarrow \begin{array}{l} (x-y)(x+y) = 12^2 \\ x + y = 18 \end{array} \Rightarrow \begin{array}{l} x - y = 8 \\ x + y = 18 \end{array} \Rightarrow$

$y = 5$.

The area is $\dfrac{2y \times 12}{2} = 12y = 12 \times 5 = 60$.

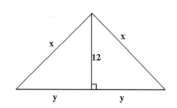

15. Solution: 41.
The area of this pentagon is equal to

$A = \dfrac{1}{2}\begin{vmatrix} 0 & 0 \\ 1 & 7 \\ 6 & 8 \\ 10 & 3 \\ 2 & 2 \\ 0 & 0 \end{vmatrix} = \dfrac{1}{2}(0 \times 7 + 1 \times 8 + 6 \times 3 + 10 \times 2$

$+ 2 \times 0 - 0 \times 1 - 7 \times 6 - 8 \times 10 - 3 \times 2 - 2 \times 0)$

$= \dfrac{1}{2} \times |46 - 128| = 41 = 41$.

16. Solution: $2\pi - 4$.
Since $\angle DBE = 90°$, DE is the diameter of the circle.
$PA = PC = PB = 4$. PB is also the diameter of the circle so $DE = 4$ and $OB = 2$. So the areas of triangle DBE equals $\dfrac{4 \times 2}{2} = 4$, and the shaded area is

$\dfrac{\pi \times 2^2}{2} - 4 = 2\pi - 4$.

17. Solution: 11.
Let O represent Pedro's pencils, R represent Peter's pencils, and L represent Paul's pencils. According to the problem,

$$O = R + 12 \qquad (1)$$
$$R = 9 + L \qquad (2)$$

1996 Mathcounts National Sprint Round Solution

We want to calculate
$$O - \frac{O+R+L}{3} = \frac{2O-R-L}{3}$$

The desired answer will be: $\frac{2O-R-L}{3} = \frac{2(R+12)-R-L}{3} = \frac{24+R-L}{3} = \frac{24+9}{3} = 11.$

18. Solution: 8.
Method 1:
As shown in the figure below, connect CD such that D is the middle point of AC. The three medians divide the triangle into six regions with the same area, so the area of triangle APC is one third of the area of triangle ABC, which is 24/3 =8.

Method 2:
Connect MN and MN = 5 and MN // AC.
Let the area of $\triangle MNP$ be x. So the area of $\triangle ACP$ is $4x$.
The area of $\triangle MNB$ is 6.

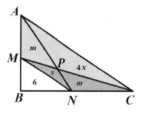

$S_{\triangle AMC} = S_{\triangle AMP} + S_{\triangle APC} = m + 4x = \frac{1}{2} AM \times BC = \frac{1}{2} \times 3 \times 8 = 12$

So $m + 4x = 12$ \hfill (1)

We see that $S_{\triangle MNB} = S_{\triangle MNC} = 6$

So $m + x = 6$ \hfill (2)

(1) – (2): $3x = 6$ $\Rightarrow$ $x = 2$ $\Rightarrow$ $4x = 8$.

19. Solution: 16.
Let c be the longest side of the triangle and the perimeter be $P = a+b+c$, where the other two sides of the triangles are a and b.

By the triangle inequality, $a + b > c$, which means that $P > 2c$ or $c < 40$.
Let $c = 39$. Then $a = 25$ and $b = 16$.

20. Solution: $\frac{25}{8}$.

Because the equation has a real solution, the determinant must be greater than or equal to 0, or $\Delta = \sqrt{b^2 - 4ac} \geq 0$

$\Delta = \sqrt{25 - 4 \times 2c} \geq 0.$

1996 Mathcounts National Sprint Round Solution

Solving for c by squaring both sides we get $c \leq \frac{25}{8}$. The greatest value of c is $\frac{25}{8}$.

21. Solution: $\frac{71}{72}$.

We know that $\frac{m}{n} < \frac{m+k}{n+k}$ for a proper fraction and positive integer k. Thus
$\frac{1}{2} < \frac{2}{3} < \frac{3}{4} < \frac{4}{5}$. The greater the denominator and the numerator, the closer the fraction is close to 1, so we place 9 and 8 as two denominators. So far, we have the sum of the fractions as $\frac{a}{9} + \frac{b}{8} = \frac{8a+9b}{72}$.
We want $8a + 9b$ to be as close to 72 as possible, so we set $8a + 9b$ to 71 to see if we are able to find values of a and b. That is, $8a + 9b = 71$
So $b = 7$ and $a = 1$ satisfies the equation, and the desired solution is
$\frac{a}{9} + \frac{b}{8} = \frac{8a+9b}{72} = \frac{71}{72}$.

22. Solution: $\frac{41}{60}$.

Method 1:
$P = \frac{24+16+18+24}{\binom{16}{2}} = \frac{82}{120} = \frac{41}{60}$.

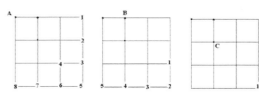

Method 2:
There are three critical points in this 4 by 4 grid: points A, B, and C, shown by the figure below.

There are four such points similar to A (corner points); eight points similar to B (2 on each side), and four points similar to C (4 points in the center).
First, we find the probability of choosing point A and then choosing a point that is farther away from point A by more than 2.5. There are 8 such points, shown in the left-most figure above. The probability is $P_1 = \frac{4}{16} \times \frac{8}{15}$.

1996 Mathcounts National Sprint Round Solution

Similarly for points B and C, we have: $P_2 = \frac{8}{16} \times \frac{5}{15}$ and $P_3 = \frac{4}{16} \times \frac{1}{15}$.

Since selection of points A, B, and C are independent to each other, so the total probability that the distance between two points is greater than 2.5 is then

$$P_1 + P_2 + P_3 = \frac{4}{16} \times \frac{8}{15} + \frac{8}{16} \times \frac{5}{15} + \frac{4}{16} \times \frac{1}{15} = \frac{19}{60}.$$

So the desired solution is: $1 - \frac{19}{60} = \frac{41}{60}$.

23. Solution: $R\sqrt{2} - R$.

From the figure above and the Pythagorean Theorem,
$(R-r)^2 = r^2 + r^2 \Rightarrow r^2 + 2rR - R^2 = 0$

$r_{1,2} = \frac{-b \pm \sqrt{b^2 - 4ac}}{2a} = \frac{-2R \pm \sqrt{(2R)^2 - 4 \times 1 \times (-R^2)}}{2}$

$= -R \pm \sqrt{2}R$.

Thus $r = R\sqrt{2} - R$.

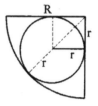

24. Solution: 56.

There are 8 vertices, and it takes 3 vertices to construct a triangle. There are $\binom{8}{3} = 56$ triangles.

25 Solution:
Let the radius of the circle O be R, the radius of the circle Q be r_1, and the radius of the circle S be r_2. We know that $r_1 = \frac{R}{2}$.

By the Pythagorean Theorem,
$(R-r_2)^2 = r_1^2 + (r_1+r_2)^2 \Rightarrow R^2 - 2Rr_2 = 2r_1r_2 \Rightarrow$

$R^2 - 2Rr_2 = 2r_1r_2 \Rightarrow r_2 = \frac{R}{3}$

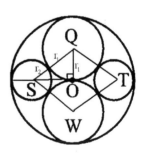

The ratio of the areas of the smallest circle and largest circle is $\frac{\pi r_2^2}{\pi R^2} = \frac{r_2^2}{R^2} = \frac{(\frac{R}{3})^2}{R^2} = \frac{1}{9}$

1996 Mathcounts National Sprint Round Solution

26. Solution: $16\frac{1}{4}$.

Let V_w be Franz's walking speed, V_r be her running speed, and D be the distance between her school and home.

It takes her x more minutes than usual to get to school after running back home to get her calculator and then running back to school.

$$x = \frac{\frac{D}{2}}{V_W} + \frac{\frac{D}{2}}{V_r} + 5 + \frac{D}{V_r} - 45 \qquad (1)$$

This is the value we are looking for.

From the distance-rate formula, $V_W = \frac{D}{45}; V_r = 2V_R = \frac{2D}{45}$.

Substituting V_w and V_r into (1), we get

$$\frac{\frac{D}{2}}{\frac{D}{45}} + \frac{\frac{D}{2}}{\frac{2D}{45}} + 5 + \frac{D}{\frac{2D}{45}} - 45 = \frac{45}{2} + \frac{45}{4} + 5 + \frac{45}{2} - 45 = 5 + \frac{45}{4} = 16\frac{1}{4}.$$

27. Solution: 8.
After graphing the inequality, we get the figure below.

The shaded area is equal to the difference between the areas of the two triangles: $\frac{5^2}{2} - \frac{3^3}{2} = \frac{16}{2} = 8$.

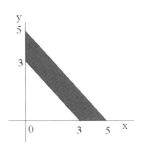

28. Solution: 495.
Let the three-digit number be $n = \overline{abc}$ and the interchanged value be $m = \overline{cba}$.
Their difference equals
$n - m = \overline{abc} - \overline{cba} = 100a + 10b + c - 100c - 10b - a = 99a - 99c = 99(a - c)$.
We are given that $450 < 99(a - c) < 550 \Rightarrow \frac{50}{11} < a - c < \frac{50}{9}$.
Since the difference $a - c$ is an integer, the only possible value is $a - c = 5$. Thus, $n - m = 495$.

1996 Mathcounts National Sprint Round Solution

29. Solution: $\dfrac{125}{12}\sqrt{2}$.

Method 1:
The tetrahedron is shown below.

The area of the base (equilateral triangle) is $A_B = \dfrac{1}{4}a^2\sqrt{3}$.

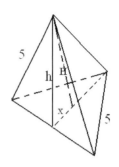

The height of the base is $h = \dfrac{1}{2}a\sqrt{3}$.

$x = \dfrac{1}{3}h = \dfrac{1}{6}a\sqrt{3}$. A is the length of one side.

The tetrahedron's height is equal to

$H = \sqrt{h^2 - x^2} = \sqrt{(\dfrac{1}{2}a\sqrt{3})^2 - (\dfrac{1}{3}\times\dfrac{1}{2}a\sqrt{3})^2} = \dfrac{\sqrt{6}}{3}a$.

The volume of the tetrahedron can be found by multiplying its height, H, with its base, A_B, which denotes the area of the equilateral triangle with side length 5.

$V = \dfrac{1}{3}A_B H = \dfrac{1}{3}\times\dfrac{1}{4}a^2\sqrt{3}\times\dfrac{\sqrt{6}}{3}a = \dfrac{\sqrt{2}}{12}a^3 = \dfrac{\sqrt{2}}{12}\times 5^3 = \dfrac{125}{12}\sqrt{2}$.

Method 2:
By the formula, the volume of a tetrahedron with side length a is equal to

$V = \dfrac{1}{3}A_B H = \dfrac{\sqrt{2}}{12}a^3 = \dfrac{\sqrt{2}}{12}\times 5^3 = \dfrac{125}{12}\sqrt{2}$.

30. Solution: 185.
The problem is the same as finding the number of non-negative solutions of

$x + y + z = 5 \qquad \Rightarrow \dbinom{7}{2}$

$x + y + z = 6 \qquad \Rightarrow \dbinom{8}{2}$

$x + y + z = 7 \qquad \Rightarrow \dbinom{9}{2}$

$x + y + z = 8 \qquad \Rightarrow \dbinom{10}{2}$

1996 Mathcounts National Sprint Round Solution

$x + y + z = 9 \quad\Rightarrow \binom{11}{2}$

There are

$\binom{7}{2} + \binom{8}{2} + \binom{9}{2} + \binom{10}{2} + \binom{11}{2} = \binom{12}{3} - \binom{6}{2} - \binom{5}{2} - \binom{4}{2} - \binom{3}{2} - \binom{2}{2} = 220 - 35 = 185$ four-digit numbers greater than 5000 where the thousands digit is equal to the sum of the other three digits.

Note: Hockey Stick Theorem
$\binom{2}{2} + \binom{3}{2} + \binom{4}{2} + \ldots + \binom{n+1}{2} = \binom{n+2}{3}$

1996 Mathcounts National Target Round Solution

1. Solution: 15.81.
Label the pentagon as shown in the figure to the right. *BD* is the longest distance between any two vertices of the pentagon. From the Pythagorean Theorem, *BD* = $\sqrt{DA^2 + BA^2}$. Since angle *C* is equivalent to angle *E*, triangle *CDE* is an isosceles right triangle. So $DG = CG = (1/2)\ CE = 5$.
$DA = DG + GA = 15$.
$BD = \sqrt{15^2 + 5^2} = \sqrt{150} = 15.81$.

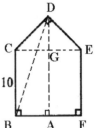

2. Solution: 15.
The common ratio of the geometric series above is $r = \dfrac{3.6}{6} = \dfrac{2.16}{3.6} = 0.6$.
The total sum of the infinite geometric series $= \dfrac{a_1}{1-r} = \dfrac{6}{1-0.6} = 15$.

3. Solution: $\dfrac{4}{5}$.

We list out all the partitions of 7:

7 = 7
= 6 + 1   = 5 + 1 + 1   = 4 + 1 + 1 + 1   = 3 + 1 + 1 + 1 + 1
= 5 + 2   = 4 + 2 + 1   = 3 + 2 + 1 + 1   = 2 + 2 + 1 + 1 + 1
= 4 + 3   = 3 + 3 + 1   = 2 + 2 + 2 + 1   = 2 + 1 + 1 + 1 + 1 +1
                    = 3 + 2 + 2
= 2 + 1 + 1 + 1 + 1 +1   = 1 + 1 + 1 + 1 + 1 + 1 + 1

Out of the 15 total partitions of 7, 12 contain a prime number.
The probability that a randomly selected partition of 7 contains a prime number is equal to $P = \dfrac{12}{15} = \dfrac{4}{5}$.

4. Solution: $x = \dfrac{5}{7}$.

We can rewrite the given inequality as: $\dfrac{14}{20} \leq \dfrac{a}{b} \leq \dfrac{16}{22}$.

Note that: $\dfrac{m}{n} \leq \dfrac{m+1}{n+1}$.

1996 Mathcounts National Target Round Solution

There is one value in between $\frac{14}{20}$ and $\frac{16}{22}$: $\frac{a}{b} = \frac{15}{21} = \frac{5}{7}$. So the fraction in the interval with the smallest denominator is $x = \frac{5}{7}$.

5. Solution: 39.
Looking at the figure on the right,
We know that $SN = SM = 4$. By Pythagorean's Theorem,
$MN = 4\sqrt{2}$.
We can also find out that
$SP = 2\sqrt{2}$, $SU = 8\sqrt{2}$, and $OU = r\sqrt{2}$.
$SU - SP - r = r\sqrt{2}$
$\Rightarrow 8\sqrt{2} - 2\sqrt{2} - r = r\sqrt{2}$
$\Rightarrow r = \frac{6\sqrt{2}}{1+\sqrt{2}}$.

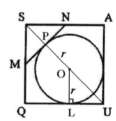

The area of the circle inscribed is equal to $\pi r^2 = \pi(\frac{6\sqrt{2}}{1+\sqrt{2}})^2 = 38.81 \approx 39$.

6. Solution: $\frac{2}{9}$.

The midpoint of any two corner points (A, B, C, and D) will be in the set S. There are $\binom{4}{2} = 6$ ways to choose two points from A, B, C, and D.
EG and HF also have midpoints within S, becoming an additional 2 ways.
The probability that the midpoint of two points selected from the nine-point set is in set S is $P = \frac{6+2}{\binom{9}{2}} = \frac{8}{36} = \frac{2}{9}$.

7. Solution: 11.
$\triangle ABC \sim \triangle CDE$ because $\angle ABC = \angle CDE$ and $\angle BCA + \angle DCE = \angle DCE + \angle DEC = 90°$
$\Rightarrow \angle BCA = \angle DEC$. Thus, $\frac{BC}{DE} = \frac{AB}{CD} \rightarrow \frac{4}{DE} = \frac{AB}{9}$.

1996 Mathcounts National Target Round Solution

Since $DE = AB$, we have $DE = 6$. By Pythagorean's Theorem,
$CE = \sqrt{9^2 + 6^2} = 10.816 \approx 11$ mm.

8. Solution: $13,500.
Dr. Martinez has had the car for 3 years, or 3×12 months. Because she had to pay $0.15 per mile for all miles driven in excess of 45,000, she must pay a total of
$0.15 \times (55240 - 45000)$.
Additionally, she must pay a down payment of $1200 and $299 per month. In total, the cost of the lease is
$1200 + 299 \times 12 \times 3 + 0.15 \times (55240 - 45000) = \$13,500$.

1997 Mathcounts National Sprint Round Solution

1. Solution: 7.
It takes 5 minutes to cook 8 hamburgers. So it will take x hours to cook 672 hamburgers, where x satisfies
$\dfrac{8}{\frac{5}{60}} = \dfrac{672}{x}$. Cross multiply and divide the resulting equation by 8 to get $x = 7$.

2. Solution: 8.
Applying the Triangle Inequality, we get
$x < 6 + 5 = 11$ $\Rightarrow$ The greatest value of x is $x = 10$.
$6 < 5 + x$ $\Rightarrow$ The least value of x is $x = 2$.
The difference is $10 - 2 = 8$.

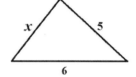

3. Solution: 12.
Method 1:
In order for the number $47\underline{x}21$ to be divisible by 3, the sum of the digits must be divisible by 3, or $4 + 7 + x + 2 + 1 \equiv 0 \mod 3$ $\Rightarrow$ $x \equiv 1 \mod 3$
x can be 1, 4, and 7. The sum of all possible digits is $1 + 4 + 7 = 12$.

Method 2:
In order for the number $47\underline{x}21$ to be divisible by 3, the sum of the digits must be divisible by 3, or $4 + 7 + x + 2 + 1 = 14 + x$ must equal 15, 18, or 21. x then equals 1, 4, or 7. The sum of all x's is 12.

4. Solution: -66.
Plugging in 8 and $2\sqrt{2}$ as x into the given function, we get
$f(8) + f(2\sqrt{2}) = 8^{\frac{2}{3}} - 8^2 + (2\sqrt{2})^{\frac{2}{3}} - (2\sqrt{2})^2 = 4 - 64 + 2 - 8 = -66$.

5. Solution: $4 + 4\sqrt{37}$.
Let the base of the triangle be $2b$. The area of the triangle equals
$24 = \dfrac{2b \times 12}{2}$.
Solve for b, $b = 2$.

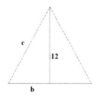

1997 Mathcounts National Sprint Round Solution

Using the Pythagorean Theorem, $c = \sqrt{12^2 + 2^2} = 2\sqrt{37}$.
The perimeter of the triangle is $2b + 2c = 4 + 4\sqrt{37}$.

6. Solution: 21.
$4^{12} \times 5^{20} = 2^{24} \times 5^{20} = 2^4 \times (2^{20} \times 5^{20}) = 1.6 \times 10^{21}$.
The exponent of 10 is 21.

7. Solution: 73%.
Let the dimensions of the box be x, y, and z. The volume is equal to $V = xyz$.
The new volume after the dimensions are increased by 20% is
$V_1 = 1.2^3 xyz = 1.728V = V + 0.728V \approx V + \dfrac{73}{100}V$.
The percent increase in volume is 73%.

8. Solution: $46\dfrac{2}{3}\%$.
Let n be the number of n&n's in the first jar. It follows that there are $0.4n$ purple n&n's. The second jar contains 50%, or half, as many n&n's as the first jar, or $0.5n$ n&n's, $0.6 \times 0.5n$ of which are purple. The total number of n&n's in both jars is $n + 0.5n = 1.5n$. Among these $1.5n$ n&n's, $0.4n + 0.6 \times 0.5n$ are purple.
So, $\dfrac{0.4n + 0.6 \times 0.5n}{n + .5n} = \dfrac{0.7}{1.5} = 46\dfrac{2}{3}\%$ of the n&n's are purple.

9. Solution: $3\dfrac{3}{4}$.
Let the ten sides of five slices of bread be A_1, B_1; A_2, B_2; A_3, B_3; A_4, B_4; A_5, B_5.
We toast the slices in the following order: A_1, A_2; A_3, A_4; A_5, B_1; B_2, B_3; and B_4, B_5 so that we can achieve the least number of toasting minutes.
In this order, it takes 45 seconds to toast one side of two slices of bread. The least number of minutes required to toast both sides of five slices of bread is $5 \times 45 = 225$ seconds $= 3\dfrac{3}{4}$ minutes.

1997 Mathcounts National Sprint Round Solution

10. Solution: 16.
Let x be the length of the side of larger square and y be the length of the side of the smaller one of the two inner squares.
The area of the shaded region is 71, so
$12 \times 8 - (x^2 + y^2) = 71 \quad \Rightarrow \quad x^2 + y^2 = 25 = 5^2 = 3^2 + 4^2$.
The larger area of the two will then be 16.

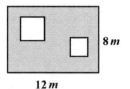

11. Solution: $\dfrac{25}{4}\pi$.

The square has a side of 5. Using the Pythagorean Theorem, the diameter of the circle circumscribed about the square is $d = \sqrt{5^2 + 5^2} = 5\sqrt{2}$.
The area of the circle is A =
$\dfrac{1}{4}\pi d^2 = \dfrac{1}{4}\pi (5\sqrt{2})^2 = \dfrac{50}{4}\pi = \dfrac{25}{4}\pi$.

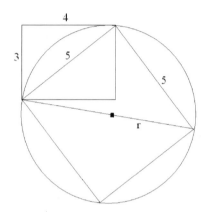

12. Solution: 7.

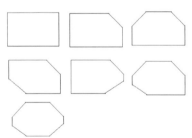

As shown in the figure above, there are 7 different denominations.

13. Solution: 8.2.
The volume of the water in the aquarium plus the volume of the solid steel cube equals
$16 \times 9 \times 8 + 3 \times 3 \times 3 = 16 \times 9 \times (8 + x) \Rightarrow 27 = 16 \times 9 \times x \Rightarrow x = 0.1875$.
The new water level is $8 + 0.1875 \approx 8.2$ inches high.
Note: We could also set $16 \times 9 \times 8 + 3 \times 3 \times 3 = 16 \times 9 \times y$ and solve for y directly to obtain the answer.

1997 Mathcounts National Sprint Round Solution

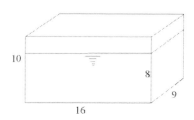
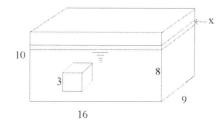

14. Solution: 999.
First we calculate how many terms in the series, ignoring the plus and minus signs.
$1997 = 1 + (n-1) \times 2 \quad \Rightarrow \quad n = 999$. There are 999 terms in the sequence.
Next, we group the terms in the way shown below:
$1 + (-3+5) + (-7+9) + \ldots + (-1995+1997)$.
Since there are a total 999 terms, there are $1 + (999-1)/2 = 1 + (499 \text{ groups})$, or
$1 + (-3+5) + (-7+9) + \ldots + (-1995+1997)$
$= 1 + \underbrace{2 + 2 + \ldots + 2}_{4992} = 1 + 2 \times 499 = 2 \times (500-1) + 1 = 1000 - 1$
$= 999$.

15. Solution: 12.
Using the Shoe-Lace theorem, where (x_1, y_1) represents point A, (x_2, y_2) represents point B, and (x_3, y_3) represents point C, the area of the triangle is

$$A = \frac{1}{2}\begin{vmatrix} x_1 & y_1 \\ x_2 & y_2 \\ x_3 & y_3 \\ x_1 & y_1 \end{vmatrix} = \frac{1}{2}\left((x_1y_2 + x_2y_3 + x_3y_1) - (x_1y_3 + x_3y_2 + x_2y_1)\right) = 12.$$

16. Solution: 171.
We first find the number of three-digit integers such that 5 is not in any of the digits, and then subtract the result from the total number of three-digit numbers.
Case I: 5 is not in the hundreds digit: $1 \times 9 \times 9 = 81$
Case II: 5 is not in the units digit: $8 \times 9 \times 9 = 648$
The answer is $900 - 648 - 81 = 171$.

1997 Mathcounts National Sprint Round Solution

17. Solution: 120.
Let B represent the amount of money Bill has, and N represent the amount of money Nancy has.
According to the problem,
$$B - 10 = N + 10$$
$$B + 10 = 2(N - 10)$$
Solve for N by subtracting the second equation from the third to get $N = 50$, and B follows as $B = 70$. $B + N = 120$.

18. Solution: 72.
We can count the number of ways where Major Domo sits next to Big Kahuna and subtract the value from the total number of ways to arrange the 5 people. There are 5! total ways to arrange the 5 people without restriction. If we think of Domo and Kahuna as one unit, we have 4!×2 ways to arrange the sitting (Note the 2 in 4!×2 signifies the swapping of positions). The number of arrangements where Major Domo is not sitting next to Big Kahuna is then 5! – 4!×2 = 72.

19. Solution: $108\sqrt{3}$.
Method 1:
Triangle ODC is a 30 – 60 – 90 triangle, so $OD = 12/2 = 6$. From the Pythagorean Theorem, $CD = \sqrt{12^2 - 6^2} = 6\sqrt{3}$ and $BC = 12\sqrt{3}$ follows.

The area of the equilateral triangle with side $12\sqrt{3}$ equals
$$A = \frac{\sqrt{3}}{4}a^2 = \frac{\sqrt{3}}{4}(12\sqrt{3})^2 = 108\sqrt{3}.$$

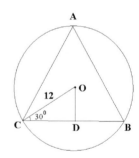

Method 2: Let AO be $2x$ and OD be x. The diameter of the circle is 12, so $2x = 12$ and $x = 6$. $AD = 3x = 18$. D is the midpoint of CB, so $AC = 2CD$. By the Pythagorean Theorem,
$$AC^2 - CD^2 = 18^2 \Rightarrow AC^2 - (\frac{1}{2}AC)^2 = 18^2 \Rightarrow AC = 12\sqrt{3}.$$

The area of the triangle is equal to $\frac{1}{2} \times 12\sqrt{3} \times 18 = 108\sqrt{3}$.

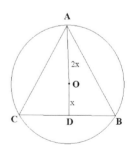

1997 Mathcounts National Sprint Round Solution

20. Solution: 7.
As shown in the figure below, after the reflection of
segment AB over the y-axis is reflected over the x-axis,
the coordinates of the midpoint of the final image
is $x = \dfrac{x_1 + x_2}{2} = \dfrac{1-5}{2} = -2$
and $y = \dfrac{y_1 + y_2}{2} = \dfrac{-2-5}{2} = -\dfrac{7}{2}$.
The product is 7.

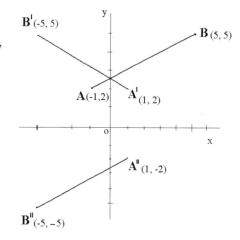

21. Solution: 16.
We are given that n is less than 48, n is integer, and n and 24 are relatively prime, meaning that n can not be a multiple of 2 or 3.

The sum of the elements of A equals $S = \dfrac{N}{24}$ where N equals the subtraction of sum of all even numbers less than 48 and the sum of all multiples of 3 less than 48 from the sum of all numbers less than 48, or

$N = \dfrac{(1+47) \times 47}{2} - (2+4+6+...+46) - 3(1+3+5+...+15) = 384$.

The desired solution is $\dfrac{384}{24} = 16$.

22. Solution: D.
$1 + 2 + 3 + 4 + ... + n = \dfrac{(1+n)n}{2} = 280 \Rightarrow \quad (1+n)n = 560$

If $n = 23$, $\dfrac{(1+23)23}{2} = 276$.

This means that the 277th term will be A, the 278th term will be B, the 279th term will be C, and the 280th term will be D.

A	B	C	D
277	278	279	280th

1997 Mathcounts National Sprint Round Solution

23. Solution: 540.
From the Pythagorean Theorem, the length of the prism is equal to 12. Looking at the figure below, we know that
$12^2 + x^2 = 15^2 \Rightarrow x = \sqrt{15^2 - 12^2} = 9$.
The volume of the rectangle with dimensions 5, 12, and 9 is equal to $12 \times 5 \times 9 = 540$.

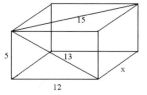

24. Solution: 200.
The nth term can be expressed as $\dfrac{1}{2n}$, so the 50th term is $\dfrac{1}{2 \times 50} = \dfrac{1}{100}$. When the 50th term is divided by the nth term, we get
$\dfrac{1}{100} \div \dfrac{1}{2n} = 4$. Solving for n, $n = 200$.

25. Solution: 16.
Let each CD's price be C and each tape's price be T.
We are given that $1.5(4C + nT) = 4T + nC$ (1)
and $C = 2T$ (2)
Substitute in $2T$ for C and solve for n, $n = 16$.

26. Solution: 6.
Let the sum of each row be S and a, b, and c be the three numbers located in the corners.
We have $1 + 2 + 3 + 4 + 5 + 6 + 7 + 8 + 9 + a + b + c = 3S$ or
$S = \dfrac{45 + a + b + c}{3}$.

The greatest sum will be $S = \dfrac{45 + 9 + 8 + 7}{3} = 23$.

The least sum will be $S = \dfrac{45 + 3 + 2 + 1}{3} = 17$.

The difference is $23 - 17 = 6$.

27. Solution: 16.
Let point P be (x, y).

1997 Mathcounts National Sprint Round Solution

$$x = \frac{x_1 + \lambda x_2}{1+\lambda} = \frac{3 + \frac{2}{3} \times 18}{1 + \frac{2}{3}} = 9 \text{ and } y = \frac{y_1 + \lambda y_2}{1+\lambda} = \frac{11 + \frac{2}{3} \times 1}{1 + \frac{2}{3}} = 7 \implies x + y = 16.$$

Note: The following relationship is true:

$$x = \frac{x_1 + \lambda x_2}{1+\lambda}, \quad y = \frac{y_1 + \lambda y_2}{1+\lambda}, \quad \lambda = \frac{\overline{AP}}{\overline{PB}} \; (-\infty < \lambda < \infty, \lambda \neq 1).$$

28. Solution: 3.
Method 1: Square both sides to get:
$(x-5)^2 > (2x-5)^2 \implies x^2 - 10x + 25 > 4x^2 - 20x + 25$
$\implies 3x^2 - 10x < 0$. The greatest integral solution is 3.

Method 2: We write the inequality as:
$\quad x - 5 > 2x - 5 \quad (1)$
$\quad x - 5 > -(2x - 5) \quad (2)$

Solve for x in (1), we get: $x > 0$.
Solve for x in (2), we get: $x < \frac{10}{3}$. The desired solution is then $x = 3$.

29. Solution: $\frac{3}{4}$.

We approach this problem using the indirect way. The integers are: 1, 2, 3, 4, 5, 6, 7, 8.
There are 7 groups that have a common prime factor: (2, 4); (2, 6); (2, 8); (3, 6), (4, 6); (4, 8); and (6, 8). The probability is $P = 1 - \frac{7}{\binom{8}{2}} = 1 - \frac{1}{4} = \frac{3}{4}$.

30. Solution: 8.
We are given the following expression
$n^{72} < 5^{96} < (n+1)^{72} \quad (1)$
Take the power of 1/24 in the expression and get:
$n^3 < 5^4 < (n+1)^3$ or $n^3 < 625 < (n+1)^3$.
We know that $8^3 = 512$ and $9^3 = 729$. Therefore, n must be 8.

1997 Mathcounts National Target Round Solution

1. Solution: 31.5.
The region determined by the above system of inequalities is equal to the area of the triangle with a base of 3 and height of 3 subtracted from a rectangle with the length of 9 and width of 4.
It's area is $9 \times 4 - \dfrac{3 \times 3}{2} = 31.5$.

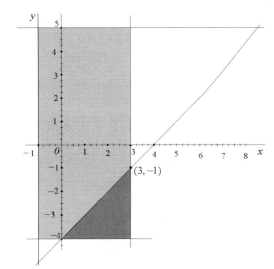

2. Solution: 67.5.
The box has a height of 1.5, width of 8 – 3, and length of 12 – 3, as shown in the figure below.
The volume is $V = 1.5 \times (8 - 3) \times (12 - 3) = 67.5$.

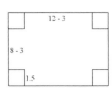

3. Solution: 727.8.
The total surface area consists of three parts: the area of the outside section, the area of inside section, and the area of top and bottom parts without the hollow parts).
The area of the outside section is $2\pi \times 1.7 \times 36$.
The area of the inside section is $2\pi \times 1.5 \times 36$.
The area of the top and bottom is $2\pi \times (1.7^2 - 1.5)^2$.
The total surface area is equal to $2\pi \times 1.7 \times 36 + 2\pi \times 1.5 \times 36 + 2\pi \times (1.7^2 - 1.5)^2 = $ 727.8 square inches.

4. Solution: 88.5.
The sum of all 25 students' scores is equal to $25 \times 82 = 2050$.
The sum of all the boys' scores is $12 \times 75 = 900$. There are 12 boys, so there are 25 – 12 = 13 girls.
The mean score of the girls equals $(2050 - 900) / 13 = 88.5$.

5. Solution: 1/6.
There are 18 integers that perfect cubes between 0 and 5000 inclusive: $0^3, 1^3, 2^3, \ldots, 17^3$ (4913).

1997 Mathcounts National Target Round Solution

Three of them are also a perfect fourth power: 0^3, 1^{12}, and $2^{12}(4096)$.
The probability is 1/6.

Note: The official answer key was 2/17 when test was given but was corrected to be 1/6 later on (because the wording "inclusive" caused confusion).

6. Solution: 41.
We labeled the figure s shown below.
$JA \times AK = 60 \times (60+120) \Rightarrow$
$AK = \sqrt{60 \times (60+120)} = 103.92$

Point A bisects chord JK. $AB = \dfrac{103.92}{2} = 51.96$.

By the Pythagorean Theorem, $GE = \sqrt{120^2 - 51.96^2} = 108.16$.
$OH = GC = \dfrac{GE + BG}{2} - 60 = \dfrac{108.16 + 60}{2} - 60 = 24.08$.

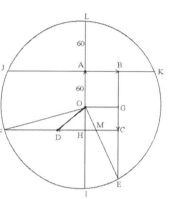

By the Pythagorean Theorem, $FH = \sqrt{120^2 - 24.08^2} = 117.56$.
$DH = DC - HC = \dfrac{FH + AB}{2} - AB = \dfrac{117.56 + 51.96}{2} - 51.96 = 32.8$
$DO = \sqrt{DH^2 + OH^2} = \sqrt{32.8^2 + 24.08^2} = 40.69 \approx 41$.

7. Solution: 2800.
Let N be the number of apples that are not perfect. We are essentially finding the number of numbers less than or equal to 6000 that are not divisible by 3, 4, or 10. Let N be the number of numbers less than or equal to 6000 that are divisible by 3, 4, or 10.

$$N = \left\lfloor \dfrac{6000}{3} \right\rfloor + \left\lfloor \dfrac{6000}{4} \right\rfloor + \left\lfloor \dfrac{6000}{10} \right\rfloor - (\left\lfloor \dfrac{6000}{3 \times 4} \right\rfloor + \left\lfloor \dfrac{6000}{3 \times 10} \right\rfloor + \left\lfloor \dfrac{6000}{LCM(4,10)} \right\rfloor) + \left\lfloor \dfrac{6000}{LCM(3,4,10)} \right\rfloor$$

$= 3200$.
We want to find the number of apples that are perfect, so the answer is $6000 - 3200 = 2800$.

8. Solution: 121.
The total area of the sidewalk equals the area of the garden, or
$\pi(r+25)^2 - \pi r^2 = \pi r^2 \Rightarrow r^2 - 50r - 25^2 = 0 \Rightarrow$
$r \neq 60.35 \Rightarrow D = 2r \approx 121$.

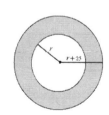

1998 Mathcounts National Sprint Round Solution

1. Solution: 50°.
$\angle ACB + 130° = 180° \Rightarrow \angle ACB = 50°$.
Since $\triangle ABC$ is isosceles, $\angle A = \angle ACB = 50° \Rightarrow$
$\angle B = 180° - 2\angle A = 180° - 100° = 50°$.

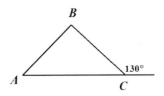

2. Solution: 72.
Factoring 225,225, we get
$225225 = 1001 \times 225 = 7 \times 11 \times 13 \times 3^2 \times 5^2$.
The number of factors is $(1 + 1)(1 + 1)(1 + 1)(2 + 1)(2 + 1) = 72$.

3. Solution: 12.5%.
The percent increase from 4.00 to 4.50 is equal to $\dfrac{4.50 - 4.00}{4.00} = 0.125 = 12.5\%$.

4. Solution: 12 days.
On the very first day, when a standard clock reads 60 minutes, the faster clock, clock B will read 60 minutes and 45 seconds. The slower clock, clock A, will read 59 minutes and 30 seconds. So, each day, the difference between the time shown on clock B and the time shown on clock A will increase by 1 minute and 15 seconds, or 1.25 minutes.
Right now, clock A is 10 minutes ahead of clock B. In order for clock B to be 5 minutes ahead of clock A, the difference between the time shown on clock B and the time shown on clock A must equal 15 minutes. Let x be the number of hours it takes for the time difference to reach 15 minutes.
$$\dfrac{1.25 \text{ minutes}}{1 \text{ day}} = \dfrac{15 \text{ minutes}}{x \text{ day}}$$
Solve for x by cross-multiplying, and we get x = 12 days.

5. Solution: 24.
Joe starts out in Albuquerque. He has 4 options for his next destination. Say he arrives at Baltimore. Then he has 3 options for his next destination. After arriving at say, Denver, he has 2 options. After stopping at say, Evanston, he has only one choice left, Cleveland, before returning back to Albuquerque. There are a total of $4 \times 3 \times 2 \times 1 \times 1 = 24$ ways.

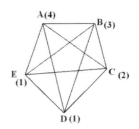

6. Solution: 100.

1998 Mathcounts National Sprint Round Solution

The filled-in square below shows a possible formation. The smallest sum is 100.

2	3	7
5	13	17
19	23	11

7. Solution: 64π.

The radius of the smallest circle is OC, where $OC = 2$.

The smallest circle is inscribed in the smaller equilateral triangle, so $OC = \frac{1}{3} BC$.

O is also the center of the middle-sized circle, so
$OB = OD = \frac{2}{3} BC = 2OC = 4$.

Using the same equilateral triangle property, $OD = \frac{1}{3} AD$ and

$OA = \frac{2}{3} AD = 2OD = 8$.

The area of the largest circle is $\pi \times 8^2 = 64\pi$.

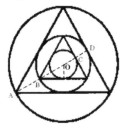

8. Solution: 12.

The last digit of this even four-digit number can only be 4. The number must be greater than 7000, so the thousands digit can be either 7 or 9, so there are two options. There are 3 choices for the hundreds digits and two choices for the tens digit.

$\underline{2} \times \underline{3} \times \underline{2} \times \underline{1} = 12$

The total number is 12.

9. Solution: 18.

Let the number of blue marbles be b and total number of green marbles be g.
According to the problem,

$\frac{g-3}{b+g-3} = \frac{2}{5} \quad \Rightarrow \quad 5g - 15 = 2b + 2g - 6 \quad \Rightarrow \quad 3g - 2b = 9$

$\frac{b+7}{b+7+g} = \frac{5}{8} \quad \Rightarrow \quad 8b + 56 = 5b + 5g + 35 \quad \Rightarrow \quad 5g - 3b = 21$

Solve the two above equations by multiplying the second equation by 3, and multiplying the first equation by 5, and subtracting the resulting equations to get $b = 18$ by eliminating g.

1998 Mathcounts National Sprint Round Solution

10. Solution: 9.
Method 1:
The product is equal to 3^{5050}.
$3^{5050} \equiv (9)^{2525} \equiv (-1)^{2525} \equiv -1 \equiv 9 \mod 10$
The units digit is 9.

Method 2:
The product is equal to 3^{5050}.

Number:	3^1	3^2	3^3	3^4
Last digit:	3	9	7	1

The pattern repeats every fourth power. So the last digit of 3^{5050} is the same as the last digit of 3^2, which is 9.

11. Solution: 490.
Method 1:
Let x be the amount of money that Brendon originally had and y be the amount of money that was returned to Brendon.
Based on our back calculation figure below, we can write the equation:
$$y \times \frac{7}{2} = \frac{5}{7}x \qquad (1)$$

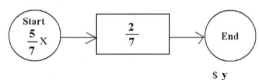

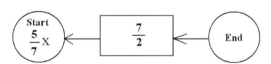

We also know that
$$\frac{2}{7}x = 40 + y. \qquad (2)$$
Solve for x using (1) and (2) by substituting in y in terms of x, and we get: $x = 490$.

Method 2:
Let O be the amount of money Brendon originally had.
$$\frac{5}{7}O - \frac{5}{7} \times \frac{5}{7}O = \frac{2}{7}O - 40 \quad \Rightarrow \quad O = 490.$$

12. Solution: $256 - 64\pi$.

1998 Mathcounts National Sprint Round Solution

The area of the un-shaded regions is equivalent to the area of four circles with radius of 4. The area of the square is equal to 16^2. So, the shaded area equals $16^2 - \pi \times r^2 \times 4 = 256 - 64\pi$.

13. Solution: 6/7.
We know that at least one child of the Wonderlich family is female, so we can rule out the option MMM. There are 7 total options, and 6 of them contain at least one male and at least one female. As shown in the figure below, the probability that at least one of the three children is a male is 6/7.

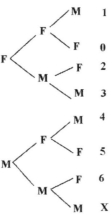

14. Solution: 12.
The expression can be simplified into $(a + b)^2 = 144$. The greatest value for $a + b$ is 12.

15. Solution: $40.
Let C be the amount of money Chen has and E be the amount of money Elyse has. According to the problem, $C - 5 = E + 5$ and $C + 5 = 3(E - 5)$.
To get E, subtract the first equation from the second and $E = 15$. C follows as 25. So, together, Chen and Elyse have $C + E = \$40$.

16. Solution: 75.
Let a be the weight of the two smaller dogs and b be the weight of the larger dog. The combined weight of three basset hounds is 185 and the difference between the weights of the larger dog and smaller dog is 20, so $2a + b = 185$ and $b - a = 20$.
Solve for b by multiplying the second equation by 2 and adding the resulting expression with the first equation, we get: $b = 75$.

1998 Mathcounts National Sprint Round Solution

17. Solution: 48.

The side of the square is $h = \frac{1}{2}a\sqrt{3} = \frac{1}{2} \times 8 \times \sqrt{3} = 4\sqrt{3}$

The area of the square is $h^2 = (4\sqrt{3})^2 = 48$.

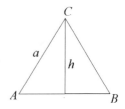

18. Solution: 24.
Let the distance biked on the first day be x.
We are given that
$x + 2x + 3x + 4x + 5x + 6x = 52 \quad \Rightarrow \quad 21x = 504 \quad \Rightarrow \quad x = 24$ miles

19. Solution: 25.
Let a, b, and c represent the area of the region each letter is in. We know that FH and EG bisect each other ($AEIF \sim CGIH$, and $FBGI \sim HDEI$).
$2b + 2c + 4a = 14 \times 8$ and $b = 15$, $c = 9$.
We can conclude that $a = 16$.
The area of the shaded region is equal to $a + c = 16 + 9 = 25$.

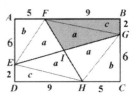

20. Solution: 332.
In order for a number to have 9 divisors, the exponents of the prime factors of the number must be either 8, or 2 and 2. ($9 = 1 \times 9 = 3 \times 3$)
$2^8 = 256$ is greater than 200, so we may rule out that option.
$2^2 \times 3^2 = 36$; $2^2 \times 5^2 = 100$; $3^2 \times 5^2 = 225$ (over 200); $2^2 \times 7^2 = 196$.
The sum is $36 + 100 + 196 = 332$.

21. Solution: 2.
Let the two numbers be a and b where $a > b$.
The sum of the two numbers is two more than their positive difference, so
$a + b = a - b + 2 \quad \Rightarrow \quad b = 1$
Since $a > b$ and in order to achieve the product of the least two positive integers, we let a be 2.
The product is $2 \times 1 = 2$.

22. Solution: 16.
Let the length of the side of the original square be a and the length of the side of the resulting square follows as $0.75a$.

1998 Mathcounts National Sprint Round Solution

$(0.75a)^2 = a^2 - 7 \implies a^2 = 16.$
The area of the original square is 16.

23. Solution: 0.
Method 1:
The common difference of this arithmetic sequence is equal to $((-20) - 5)/5 = -5$.
Therefore a_4 is $5 - 5 = 0$. The product of the 4th term and any term in the sequence is 0.

Method 2:
$$a_n = a_1 + (n-1)d$$
$$5 = a_1 + (5-1)d$$
$$-20 = a_1 + (8-1)d$$
Solve the system equations to get: $d = -5 \implies a_4 = 0$.
The product of the 4th term and any term in the sequence is 0.

24. Solution: $\dfrac{7}{30}$.

There are 3 cards with vowels: A, O, and U and 7 cards containing consonants: M, T, H, C, N, T, and S.
The probability that the first card chosen has a vowel on it is $\dfrac{3}{10}$.
The probability that the second card chosen has a consonant on it is $\dfrac{7}{9}$.
The desired answer is: $P = \dfrac{3}{10} \times \dfrac{7}{9} = \dfrac{7}{30}$.

25. Solution: 22.
The smaller triangle has an area of 100 square feet, so $S_S = 100$. Let S_L denote the area of the larger triangle. The ratio of the areas of two similar triangles is the square of the ratio of their corresponding sides, or $\dfrac{S_L}{S_S} = (\dfrac{2}{3})^2$.
Since $S_S = 100$, $S_L = (\dfrac{3}{2})^2 \times 100 = 225$.

1998 Mathcounts National Sprint Round Solution

26. Solution: $\frac{27}{2}\sqrt{3}$.

The figure shows six shaded small triangles and 16 small triangles in total.

The area of the each small triangle, where each side is 12/4 = 3 inches long, is equal to $S = \frac{1}{4}a^2\sqrt{3} = \frac{1}{4} \times 3^2 \times \sqrt{3} = \frac{9}{4}\sqrt{3}$.

The total area of six such triangles, the shaded portion, is equal to $6 \times \frac{9}{4}\sqrt{3} = \frac{27}{2}\sqrt{3}$.

27. Solution: 96.
he perimeter of the rectangle is equal to $2(2a + 10) + 2(2a) = 44 \Rightarrow a = 8$.
Looking at the figure to the right, we can see that the area of the rectangle can be found by $(2a + 10) \times 2a$.

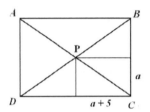

Substitute in a into the expression above to get the number of square centimeters in the area of the rectangle: $(2a + 10) \times 2a = 96$.

28. Solution: 3.
A scalene triangle is a triangle with no equal side lengths. Let the third side of this triangle be x.
From the Triangle Inequality, we can say that
$3 + 5 > x \quad \Rightarrow \quad x < 8$. We have three such lengths for x: $x = 7$, $x = 6$, and $x = 4$.
From the Triangle Inequality, we can also say that $5 + x > 3$. However, this isn't very helpful.
So we have 3 such lengths for the third side: 7, 6, and 4.

29. Solution: 168.
Method 1: We are given that
$M + P^2 = 7308$ (1)
$M^2 + P = 6974$ (2)

(1) − (2) ⇒
$P^2 - M^2 + M - P = 334 \quad \Rightarrow \quad (P-M)(P+M) - (P-M) = 334$
$\Rightarrow (P-M)(P+M-1) = 2 \times 167$.

1998 Mathcounts National Sprint Round Solution

$P + M - 1 = 167 \Rightarrow P + M = 168$.

Method 2: We are given that
$$M + P^2 = 7308 \qquad (1)$$
$$M^2 + P = 6974 \qquad (2)$$
Since P and M are both positive integers, from (1), we know that $P \leq 85$ and from (2), we know that $M \leq 83$.
Substitute the value of P, 85, into (1), to get $M = 83$.
$P = 85$ and $M = 83$ also satisfies equation (2), so our answer is $85 + 83 = 168$.

30. Solution: $1,600,000.
Because the amount received is proportional to the amount invested, Beth's share of winnings is $\dfrac{20}{25 + 20 + 35} \times 6,400,000 = \$1,600,000$.

1998 Mathcounts National Target Round Solution

1. Solution: $\dfrac{46}{35}$.

$$\cfrac{1}{1+\cfrac{1}{1+\cfrac{1}{1+1}}} = \cfrac{1}{1+\cfrac{1}{1+\cfrac{1}{2}}} = \cfrac{1}{1+\cfrac{1}{\frac{3}{2}}} = \cfrac{1}{1+\frac{2}{3}} = \cfrac{1}{\frac{5}{3}} = \frac{3}{5}.$$

Similarly: $\cfrac{2}{2+\cfrac{2}{2+\cfrac{2}{2+2}}} = \dfrac{5}{7}.$

The answer is $\dfrac{5}{7}+\dfrac{3}{5}=\dfrac{46}{35}.$

2. Solution: 22.1.

The sum of the lengths of the edges of the tetrahedron equals $2 + 3 + 4 + AB + BC + AC$
$= 9 + \sqrt{2^2+3^2} + \sqrt{2^2+4^2} + \sqrt{3^2+4^2} \approx 22.078 \approx 22.1.$

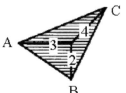

3. Solution: $\dfrac{2}{3}$.

Let A and B be the two players who show the same sign and C be the player who shows a different sign. A has three choices, B has 1, and C has 2.

$\quad\quad A \quad\quad B \quad\quad C$
$\quad\quad 3 \,\times\, 1 \,\times\, 2 = 6$ ways.

Players A and C can also show the same sign, and so can players B and C. So we have $6 \times 3 = 18$ ways.

The total number of options is $3 \times 3 \times 3 = 27$.

The probability that two players show the same sign is $P = \dfrac{18}{27} = \dfrac{2}{3}.$

1998 Mathcounts National Target Round Solution

4. Solution: 103.

If it takes 0.4 seconds for the ball to travel 60.6 feet, then it takes 1 second for the ball to travel 60.6/0.4 feet. In miles per hour, the ball traveled at the speed of

$$\frac{\frac{60.6}{0.4} \times 60 \times 60}{5280} = 103.125 = 103.$$

5. Solution: 72.
Method 1:
Triangles *ABC*, *FEB*, and *ACB* are all similar to each other, so the ratio of areas is equal to the square of the ratio of corresponding sides.

$$S_{\triangle ABC} = \frac{16 \times 12}{2} = 96.$$

The length of *BC* is 20 and the length of *EB* is 8, so

$$\frac{S_{\triangle FEB}}{S_{\triangle ABC}} = (\frac{8}{20})^2 = \frac{4}{25} \quad \Rightarrow \quad S_{\triangle FEB} = \frac{4}{25} S_{\triangle ABC}.$$

The length of *BC* is 20 and the length of *DC* is 6, so

$$\frac{S_{\triangle GCD}}{S_{\triangle ABC}} = (\frac{6}{20})^2 = \frac{9}{100} \quad \Rightarrow \quad S_{\triangle CDG} = \frac{9}{100} S_{\triangle ABC}.$$

The area of pentagon *AEFGD* is equal to

$$S_{\triangle ABC} - S_{\triangle FEB} - S_{\triangle CDG} = S_{\triangle ABC} - \frac{4}{25} S_{\triangle ABC} - \frac{9}{100} S_{\triangle ABC}$$

$$= S_{\triangle ABC}(1 - \frac{4}{25} - \frac{9}{100}) = 96 \times (\frac{100 - 16 - 9}{100}) = 72.$$

Method 2:

ABC is a 12-16-20 right triangle. Connect *DE*. $DE = \frac{1}{2} BC = 10$.

Triangles *AEF* and *GDC* are all similar to each other. So $\frac{AE}{DG} = \frac{DE}{DC}$

$$\Rightarrow \quad \frac{8}{DG} = \frac{10}{6} \quad \Rightarrow \quad DG = \frac{48}{10} = \frac{24}{5}.$$

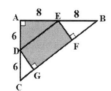

The area of pentagon *AEFGD* is $S_{\triangle ADE} + S_{DEFG} = \frac{1}{2} \times 6 \times 8 + 10 \times \frac{24}{5} = 72.$

1998 Mathcounts National Target Round Solution

6. Solution: 48.

The lowest average that Tom could have is 81.6 so that his average score rounded to the nearest integer is 82. Since we want to find x, the lowest score for the fourth test, we let the four highest scores all be 90.

$$81.6 \leq \frac{90 + 90 + 90 + x + 90}{5} \leq 82 \quad \Rightarrow \quad 48 \leq x \leq 50.$$

The smallest integer of x is 48.

Note: The lowest average that Tom could have cannot be 81.5 ($81.5 \times 5 = 407.5$ which is not an integer).

7. Solution: 4.
Method 1:
We are essentially solving the following equation: $5x + 6y + 2z = n$, where $0 \leq x \leq 10$, $0 \leq y \leq 7$, and $0 \leq z \leq 2$.

The scores of 1, 3, 97, and 99 are not possible and all other scores are possible.
4 scores are impossible to score.

Method 2:
We have $100 = 10 \times 5 + 7 \times 6 + 4 \times 2$.
When we miss questions with 2 points, at most we can get a 98, 96, 94,...
We are not able to get a 99.
When we miss questions with 5 points, at most we can get a 95.
We are not able to get a 97.
From the lower side, we are not able to get 1 and 3.
We guess that that is all we are not able to get.

Any number between 6 and 96 will be able to get:

$6k$: the greatest value is 96. $96 = 6 \times 7 + 5 \times 10 + 2 \times 2 = 6 \times 7 + 5 \times (6 + 4) + 2 \times 2 = 6 \times 7 + 6 \times 5 + 5 \times 4 + 4 = = 6 \times 7 + 6 \times 5 + 6 \times 4$

$6k + 1$: the greatest value is 91. $91 = 6 \times 7 + 5 \times 9 + 2 \times 2 = 6 \times 7 + 5 \times 6 + 5 \times 3 + 2 \times 2 = 6 \times 7 + 6 \times 5 + 6 \times 3 + 1$

$6k + 2$: the greatest value is 98. $98 = 6 \times 7 + 5 \times 10 + 3 \times 2 = 6 \times 7 + 5 \times (6 + 4) + 3 \times 2 = 6 \times 7 + 5 \times 6 + 20 + 3 \times 2 = 6 \times 7 + 5 \times 6 + 6 \times 3 + 6 + 2$

$6k + 3$: the greatest value is 93. $93 = 6 \times 7 + 5 \times 9 + 3 \times 2 = 6 \times 7 + 5 \times (6 + 3) + 6 = 6 \times$

1998 Mathcounts National Target Round Solution

$7 + 5 \times 6 + 5 \times 3 + 6 = 6 \times 7 + 5 \times 6 + 6 + 6 \times 3 + 3$

$6k + 4$: the greatest value is 94. $94 = 6 \times 7 + 5 \times 10 + 2 = 6 \times 7 + 5 \times (6 + 4) + 2 = 6 \times 7 + 5 \times 6 + 20 + 2 = = 6 \times 7 + 5 \times 6 + 6 \times 3 + 4$

$6k + 5$: the greatest value is 95. $95 = 6 \times 7 + 5 \times 9 + 4 \times 2 = 6 \times 7 + 5 \times (6 + 3) + 4 \times 2 = 6 \times 7 + 6 \times 5 + 6 \times 2 + 3 + 6 + 2 = 6 \times 7 + 6 \times 5 + 6 \times 2 + 6 + 5$.

8. Solution: 3.8.

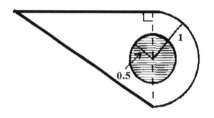

Total area of the figure above
= The area of the right triangle + the area of the semicircle = $\dfrac{\pi \times 1^2}{2} + \dfrac{3 \times 2}{2}$.

The shared area = $\pi \times (0.5)^2$.

The area of the region not shaded is $\dfrac{\pi}{2} + \dfrac{3 \times 2}{2} - \pi \times (0.5)^2 = 3.785 \approx 3.8$.

1999 Mathcounts National Sprint Round Solutions

1. Solution: $\dfrac{5}{12}$.

A 3-digit number is divisible by 3 if the sum of its digits is divisible by 3.
The first digit cannot be 0, so we have the following four groups of 3 such that the three different numbers sum to a multiple of 3:
2, 4, 0;   8, 4, 0;   6, 4, 2;   8, 6, 4.
These four cases produce 4, 4, 6, and 6 numbers respectively.
There are $4 + 4 + 6 + 6 = 20$ such numbers. There are a total of $4\times 4\times 3 = 48$ three-digit numbers using the digits 0, 2, 4, 6, and 8.
The probability is $P = \dfrac{20}{4\times 4\times 3} = \dfrac{5}{12}$.

2. Solution: 9.

A network of the cube is shown below.

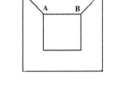

A network can be traversed without retracing any edge if it has two odd nodes. A node is one of the 8 vertices. An odd node is a vertex that has an odd number of edges coming out of it. This network has 8 odd nodes, so six such nodes need to be removed. One example is shown. The two odd nodes left with one being the starting point and the other one being the ending point. The longest distance is then 9.

3. Solution: $\dfrac{11}{18}$.

Let the event of removing a red ball be A_1, the event of removing a white ball be A_2, and the event of selecting a red ball be B. We have

$P(A_1) = \dfrac{4}{6} = \dfrac{2}{3}$ $P(B|A_1) = \dfrac{3}{6} = \dfrac{1}{2}$ (The probability of selecting a red ball after removing and replacing a red ball.)

$P(A_2) = \dfrac{2}{6} = \dfrac{1}{3}$ $P(B|A_2) = \dfrac{5}{6}$ (The probability of selecting a red ball after removing and replacing a white ball.)

$P(B) = P(A_1)\times P(B|A_1) + P(A_2)\times P(B|A_2) = \dfrac{2}{3}\times\dfrac{1}{2} + \dfrac{1}{3}\times\dfrac{5}{6} = \dfrac{1}{3} + \dfrac{5}{18} = \dfrac{11}{18}$.

1999 Mathcounts National Sprint Round Solutions

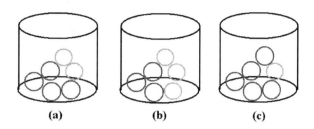

(a) (b) (c)

4. Solution: 56.
Let g be the number of girls and b be the number of boys.
According to the problem, after one-fifth of the girls left, the ratio of the girls to boys was 2:5, or

$$\frac{\frac{4}{5}g}{b}=\frac{2}{3} \quad (1) \qquad \Rightarrow \qquad \frac{4}{5}g=\frac{2}{3}b \quad (2)$$

After 44 boys leave, the ratio of boys to girls was 2:5, or

$$\frac{\frac{4}{5}g}{b-44}=\frac{5}{2} \quad (3)$$

Substituting (2) to (3): $\dfrac{\frac{2}{3}b}{b-44}=\dfrac{5}{2}$ ⇒(cross multiply) $\quad 5(b-44)=\dfrac{4}{3}b$

$\Rightarrow\ 5b-220=\dfrac{4}{3}b \quad \Rightarrow \quad 5b-\dfrac{4}{3}b=220 \quad \Rightarrow \quad \dfrac{11}{3}b=220 \quad \Rightarrow b=60.$

Substitute the value of b into any of the above equations to obtain g = 50.

The number of students who remained $=(b-44)+\dfrac{4}{5}g=(60-44)+\dfrac{4}{5}\times 50 =16+40=56.$

5. Solution: $\dfrac{3}{2}$.

The area of $\triangle BEF$ = The area of the square $ABCD$ – The area of $\triangle EDF$ – The area of $\triangle BAE$ – The areas of $\triangle BCF$

$=2^2-\dfrac{1\times 1}{2}-2\times\dfrac{1\times 2}{2}=4-\dfrac{1}{2}-2=\dfrac{3}{2}.$

6. Solution: $\dfrac{1}{5}$.

1999 Mathcounts National Sprint Round Solutions

There are a total of 15 cards. There are $\binom{15}{3}$ ways to choose 3 cards from 15. There are $\binom{8}{3}$ ways to choose 3 red cards from 8 and $\binom{7}{3}$ ways to choose 3 black cards from 7. The probability is equal to $\dfrac{\binom{8}{3}+\binom{7}{3}}{\binom{15}{3}} = \dfrac{1}{5}$.

7. Solution: 17.
Method 1:
Three lines can have 3 points of intersection. One circle will have at most 2 points of intersection with each line. So, each circle will add 6 more points and 2 circles will add 12 points of intersection with the lines. However, two circles will also have at most 2 points of intersection with themselves. This will add 2 more points of intersection. The total points of intersection among two circles and three lines are 3 + 12 +2 = 17.

Method 2:
Direct counting:

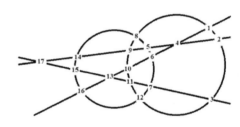

8. Solution: $12\sqrt{15}$.
Using the Heron formula to find the area of the triangle, we get
$s = \dfrac{1}{2}(a+b+c) = \dfrac{1}{2}(8+12+16) = 18$.
$A = \sqrt{s(s-a)(s-b)(s-c)} = \sqrt{18(18-8)(18-12)(18-16)} = 12\sqrt{15}$.

9. Solution: $81\sqrt{3}$.
Shown in the 2-D image below, the diameter of the sphere is the same as the side length of the large cube. The diameter of the sphere is also the same as the length of the small cube's diagonal. Let the side of the small cube be a. It's diagonal has a length of 9, so we know that $a^2 + a^2 + a^2 = 9^2$. $a = \dfrac{9}{\sqrt{3}}$ and the volume of the inscribed cube is

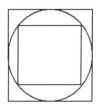

1999 Mathcounts National Sprint Round Solutions

$a^3 = (\dfrac{9}{\sqrt{3}})^3 = 81\sqrt{3}$.

10. Solution: $\dfrac{37}{64}$.

       Stage 0   Stage 1   Stage 2   Stage 3

The nine white squares in stage 2, after partially shaded, will produce $\dfrac{1}{4} \times 9$ more shaded areas. The fraction of shaded area in the third stage will be $\dfrac{7 + \dfrac{9}{4}}{16} = \dfrac{37}{64}$.

Note: See a similar problem in 1995 National Sprint problem 20.

11. Solution: 0.16.

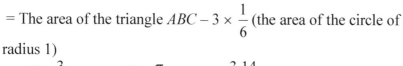

The area of $\triangle ABC$ equals $\dfrac{\sqrt{3}}{4} a^2 = \dfrac{\sqrt{3}}{4} \times 2^2 = \sqrt{3}$. The three white regions represent three pieces of one-sixth of a circle.
The area of the shaded region
= The area of the triangle $ABC - 3 \times \dfrac{1}{6}$ (the area of the circle of radius 1)
$= \sqrt{3} - \dfrac{3}{6}\pi \times 1^2 = \sqrt{3} - \dfrac{\pi}{2} = 1.737 - \dfrac{3.14}{2} = 0.16$.

12. Solution: $-\dfrac{1}{8}$.

Method 1:
Square both sides:
$(5x-1)^2 = (3x+2)^2$
$\Rightarrow 25x^2 - 10x + 1 = 9x^2 + 12x + 4$

1999 Mathcounts National Sprint Round Solutions

$16x^2 - 22x - 3 = 0$. Using the quadratic formula, we get $x_1 = \frac{3}{2}$ and $x_2 = -\frac{1}{8}$. The smallest value is $x_2 = -\frac{1}{8}$.

Method 2:
We write the equation as two equations: $5x - 1 = 3x + 2$ (1)
and $5x - 1 = -(3x + 2)$ (2)

Solve for x in (1), we get: $x = \frac{3}{2}$

Solve for x in (2), we get: $x = -\frac{1}{8}$. The desired solution is then $x = -\frac{1}{8}$.

13. Solution: 2.
$y = f(x) = \frac{4x+1}{3}$; $x = \frac{3y-1}{4}$; $f^{-1}(1) = \frac{3 \times 1 - 1}{4} = \frac{1}{2}$; $(f^{-1}(1))^{-1} = (\frac{1}{2})^{-1} = 2$.

14. Solution: 28.
Using the Triangle Inequality, we have:
$x + 8 + x + 8 > 3x - 9$ (1)
$x + 8 + 3x - 9 > x + 8$ (2)
Solve x in (1), we have $25 > x$.
Solve x in (2), we have $x > 3$.
The smallest value for x is 24 and the largest value is 4. The answer is $24 + 4 = 28$.

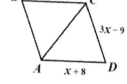

15. Solution: 10.
The radius of the circle is $26/2 = 13$. The radius of the circle is a perpendicular bisector of the chord. Using the Pythagorean Theorem, the desired solution is
$2x = 2 \times \sqrt{13^2 - 12^2} = 2 \times 5 = 10$.
Note: Some Common Pythagorean Triples:

3	4	5
5	12	13
8	15	17
7	24	25
20	21	29
12	35	37
9	40	41
11	60	61
13	84	85

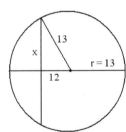

1999 Mathcounts National Sprint Round Solutions

16. Solution: 402.
Method 1:
$12 = 1 \times 2 \times 6 = 1 \times 3 \times 4 = 2 \times 2 \times 3 = 2 \times 6 = 3 \times 4$.
The 2-digit positive integers have the form of $2^{(a+1)} \times 3^{(b+1)} \times 5^{(c+1)} \times 7^{(d+1)} \cdots$
We found the following 2-digit positive integers that have 12 factors:
$2^5 \times 3^1 \times 5^0 = 96$
$2^3 \times 3^2 \times 5^0 = 72$
$2^1 \times 3^2 \times 5^1 = 90$
$2^2 \times 3^1 \times 5^1 = 60$
$2^2 \times 3^1 \times 7^1 = 84$
The desired solution is $60 + 72 + 84 + 90 + 96 = 402$.

Note:
Table of factors of counting numbers 1 to 100

Number of factors	Counting numbers	Number of counting numbers	Property
1	1	1	Square number
2	2, 3, 5, 7, 11, 13, 17, 19, 23, 29, 31, 37, 41, 43, 47, 53, 59, 61, 67, 71, 73, 79, 83, 89, 97	25	Prime number
3	4, 9, 25, 49	4	Square of a prime
4	6, 8, 10, 14, 15, 21, 22, 26, 27, 33, 34, 35, 38, 39, 46, 51, 55, 57, 58, 62, 65, 69, 74, 77, 82, 85, 86, 87, 91, 93, 94, 95	32	
5	16, 81	2	Square number
6	12, 18, 20, 28, 32, 44, 45, 50, 52, 63, 68, 75, 76, 92, 98, 99	16	
7	64	1	Square number
8	24, 30, 40, 42, 54, 56, 66, 70, 78, 88	10	
9	36, 100	2	Square number
10	48, 80	2	
11		0	
12	60, 72, 84, 90, 96	5	

1999 Mathcounts National Sprint Round Solutions

17. Solution: $\dfrac{1}{2}$.

$\triangle AOB \sim \triangle COM$ ($AB \parallel MC$). M is the midpoint of CD. $\dfrac{OC}{OA} = \dfrac{2}{4} = \dfrac{1}{2}$.

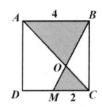

18. Solution: $\dfrac{1}{10}$.

There are $\underline{9} \times \underline{10} \times \underline{1} = 90$ 3-digit palindromes. There are $\underline{9} \times \underline{10} \times \underline{10} = 900$ 3-digit palindromes. The probability is then $P = \dfrac{90}{900} = \dfrac{1}{10}$.

19. Solution: 16.
Let the two numbers be x and y.
According to the problem,
$xy - (x+y) = 39 \quad \Rightarrow \quad (x-1)(y-1) = 40 = 10 \times 4 = 8 \times 5$.
(Note that $40 = 20 \times 2 = 40 \times 1$ are both out of range, since each number must be less than 20.)
$(x-1) = 8$ and $(y-1) = 5$ gives $x = 9$ and $y = 6$. They share 3 as a common factor, so they are not relatively prime.
$(x-1) = 10$ and $(y-1) = 4$ gives $x = 11$ and $y = 5$. The sum is 16.

20. Solution: 38.
$\dfrac{9a-8}{10a-8} = \dfrac{5}{6} \quad \Rightarrow \quad 54a - 48 = 50a - 40 \quad \Rightarrow \quad a = 2$
The sum of the original fraction's numerator and denominator is $(9+10)a = 38$.

21. Solution: $\dfrac{32}{65}$.

The total number of outcomes is equal to $\underline{15} \times \underline{14} \times \underline{13} \times \underline{12}$, since the balls are selected without replacement.
We are given 8 odd numbers (1, 3, 5, 7, 9, 11, 13, 15) and 7 even numbers (2, 4, 6, 8, 10, 12, 14).
In order to get an odd sum, we need to have the following selections of the balls:
Case I: Odd, Even, Even, Even.
There are $\underline{8} \times \underline{7} \times \underline{6} \times \underline{5} \times \dfrac{4!}{3! \times 1!}$ ways in this case.
Case II: Odd, Odd, Odd, Even.

112

1999 Mathcounts National Sprint Round Solutions

There are $8 \times 7 \times 6 \times 7 \times \dfrac{4!}{3! \times 1!}$ ways in this case.

The desired probability is $P = \dfrac{8 \times 7 \times 6 \times 5 \times \dfrac{4!}{3! \times 1!} + 8 \times 7 \times 6 \times 7 \times \dfrac{4!}{3! \times 1!}}{15 \times 14 \times 13 \times 12} = \dfrac{32}{65}$.

22. Solution: 67.
(1) The number of squares in the figure (a): $4^2 + 3^2 + 2^2 + 1^2 = 30$;
(2) The number of shaded squares consisting of one small square: 24;
(3). The number of squares consisting of 4 small squares in (c): $5 + 5 - 1 = 9$;
(4) The number of squares in (d): 4.
The total number of squares is $30 + 24 + 9 + 4 = 67$.

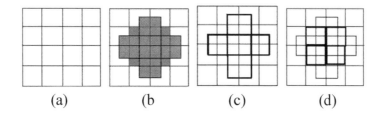

(a)   (b)   (c)   (d)

23. Solution: 4.
Method 1:
When Rachel divides her favorite number by 7, she gets a remainder of 5. The smallest value for her favorite number can be $7 + 5 = 12$. $12 \times 5 = 60$. The remainder will be 4 when 60 is divided by 7.

Method 2:
Let Rachel's favorite number be x.
Since she gets a remainder of 5 after dividing her number by 7, we have
$x \equiv 5 \mod 7$
$5x \equiv 5 \times 5 \equiv 4 \mod 7$. So the remainder will be 4.

24. Solution: $\dfrac{13}{20}$.

Let the number picked be x. According to the Triangle Inequality, we have
$\quad\quad 12 + 7 > x \quad\quad \Rightarrow \quad\quad x < 19$
$\quad\quad 7 + x > 12 \quad\quad \Rightarrow \quad\quad x > 5$

1999 Mathcounts National Sprint Round Solutions

There are a total of 20 numbers and the favorable outcomes are from 6 to 18. The probability is $P = \dfrac{18-6+1}{20} = \dfrac{13}{20}$.

25. Solution: $\dfrac{1}{3}$.

In order for the five-digit number to be divisible by 36, the number needs to be divisible by both 4 and 9. This means that the number formed by the last two digits must be divisible by 4 (the units digit must then be 2 or 6) and the sum of the digit must be divisible by 9.
We then have:

$2 + 1 + x + 7 + 2 \equiv 0 \mod 9$ $\Rightarrow$ $3 + x \equiv 0 \mod 9$ $\Rightarrow$ $x = 6$
$2 + 1 + x + 7 + 6 \equiv 0 \mod 9$ $\Rightarrow$ $x + 7 \equiv 0 \mod 9$ $\Rightarrow$ $x = 2$

The ratio of the smaller digit to the larger digit is $\dfrac{2}{6} = \dfrac{1}{3}$.

26. Solution: 5.

Let the first term of the sequence be a. The sum of first ten terms of an arithmetic sequence with a common difference of, say, 1.
$S = a + a + 1 + a + 2 + .. + a + 10 = 10a + 45 = 5(2a + 9)$.
S must be divisible by 5.

27. Solution: $\dfrac{5}{4}$.

Shown in the figure below, the area of the shaded region is equal to the areas of the two small triangles subtracted from the area of the surrounding rectangle, or

$\dfrac{\sqrt{2}}{2} \times \dfrac{3\sqrt{2}}{2} - \dfrac{\frac{1}{2} \times \frac{1}{2}}{2} \times 2 = \dfrac{5}{4}$.

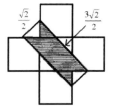

28. Solution: $\dfrac{1}{4}$.

$f(x) = \dfrac{1}{1 - \dfrac{1}{1 - \dfrac{1}{1-x}}} = \dfrac{1}{1 - \dfrac{1}{\dfrac{1-x}{1-x} - \dfrac{1}{1-x}}} = \dfrac{1}{1 - \dfrac{1}{\dfrac{-x}{1-x}}} = \dfrac{1}{1 + \dfrac{1-x}{x}} = \dfrac{1}{\dfrac{x}{x} - \dfrac{1-x}{x}} = x$.

114

1999 Mathcounts National Sprint Round Solutions

$f(-2) = -2;\quad f(f(-2)) = f(-2) = -2;\quad (f(f(-2)))^{-2} = (-2)^{-2} = \dfrac{1}{2^2} = \dfrac{1}{4}.$

29. Solution: $\dfrac{1}{128}$.

The perimeters form a pattern:

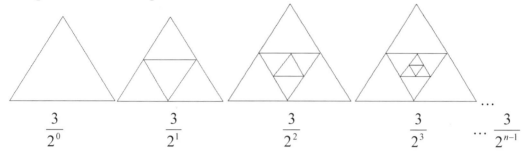

The pattern is a geometric sequence with a common ratio of $\dfrac{1}{2}$. The ratio of the perimeter of the tenth triangle to the perimeter of the third triangle is

$\dfrac{\frac{3}{2^9}}{\frac{3}{2^2}} = \dfrac{2^2}{2^9} = \dfrac{1}{2^7} = \dfrac{1}{128}.$

30. Solution: 80.

We first find the pattern of the perimeter of the arrangement as shown below, where N is the number of rows in the figure:

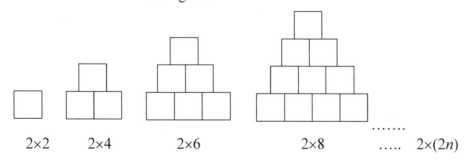

The perimeter of the figure with n rows is equal to $2 \times (2n)$.
Next, we find how many rows are in the 20th figure.

$1 + 2 + 3 + 4 + \ldots + n = \dfrac{(1+n)n}{2} = 210 \quad\Rightarrow\quad n = 20.$

The desired perimeter is $2 \times (2n) = 2 \times 2 \times 20 = 80.$

1999 Mathcounts National Target Round Solutions

1. Solution: 26.
Write the two-digit number in the form $\overline{ab} = 10a + b$. We multiply this number by 5 and adjoin a 7 to its end. The new 4-digit number is 1281 greater than the original two-digit number.
We have $(10a + b) \times 5 \times 10 + 7 = 1281 + 10a + b \quad \Rightarrow \quad 10a + b = 26$
$a = 2$ and $b = 6$.
The original number is 26.

2. Solution: September, 2022.
The time used to count to 9,999,999,999 from 2,519,206,712 if 0.1 second passes for every $1 increase is $\dfrac{9,999,999,999 - 2,519,206,712}{10 \times 60 \times 60 \times 24} = 8,658.326$ days.
$\dfrac{8,658.326}{365} = 23.72$ years.
0.72 years = 0.72 × 12 = 8.77 months.
It will take 23 years and more than 8 months. The answer is September, 2022.

3. Solution: 3.27.
The area of the semicircle with radius r is $\dfrac{\pi r^2}{2}$.

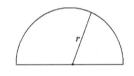

The perimeter of a semicircle with radius r is $2r + \dfrac{2\pi r}{2}$.

$\dfrac{\pi r^2}{2} = 2r + \dfrac{2\pi r}{2} \quad \Rightarrow \quad \dfrac{\pi r}{2} = 2 + \dfrac{2\pi}{2} \quad \Rightarrow \quad r = \dfrac{(4 + 2\pi)}{\pi} \approx 3.27$.

4. Solution: 36.
The abscissa is the x-coordinate. Looking at the figure below, the sum of the x-coordinates is equal to
12 + 10 + 14 = 36.

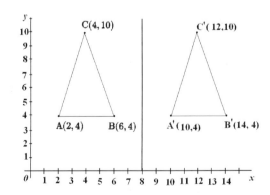

1999 Mathcounts National Target Round Solutions

5. Solution: 8.1.

The distance-speed formula states that $s = \dfrac{d}{t}$, where d is the total distance and t is the total time, and s is the average speed.

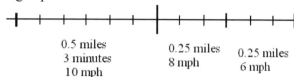

0.5 miles
3 minutes
10 mph

0.25 miles
8 mph

0.25 miles
6 mph

$$s = \dfrac{1}{\dfrac{0.5}{10} + \dfrac{0.25}{8} + \dfrac{0.25}{6}} = 8.13533 \approx 8.1 \text{ miles/hour.}$$

6. Solution: $\dfrac{1}{4}$.

We have three cases:
Case I: Rolling a cube with one side painted:
There are 24 1" by 1" by 1" cubes with one side painted.

The probability that a cube with one side painted being randomly selected is $\dfrac{24}{64}$.

The probability that the one painted face appears on the top face of the rolled cube is $\dfrac{1}{6}$.

$$\dfrac{24}{64} \times \dfrac{1}{6} = \dfrac{1}{16}.$$

Case II: Rolling a cube with two sides painted:
There are 24 1" by 1" by 1" cubes with two sides painted. The probability that the top face of the rolled cube with two sides painted is painted is
$$\dfrac{24}{64} \times \dfrac{2}{6} = \dfrac{1}{8}.$$

Case III: Rolling a cube with three sides painted:
There are 8 1" by 1" by 1" cubes with three sides painted. The probability that the top face of the rolled cube with three sides painted is painted is
$$\dfrac{8}{64} \times \dfrac{3}{6} = \dfrac{1}{16}$$

The probability that the top face of a rolled cube is painted is $P = \dfrac{1}{16} + \dfrac{1}{8} + \dfrac{1}{16} = \dfrac{1}{4}$.

Useful knowledge:

1999 Mathcounts National Target Round Solutions

Cube	Dimensions: $n \times n \times n$ ($n \geq 2$)
3 faces painted	8
2 faces painted	$(n-2)^1 \times 2 \times 6$
1 face painted	$(n-2)^2 \times 1 \times 6$
0 face painted	$(n-2)^3$
Total number of small cubes	n^3

7. Solution: 60.

Let $AB = a$, $CD = b$, $\dfrac{1}{EF} = \dfrac{1}{a} + \dfrac{1}{b}$.

$\dfrac{1}{EF} = \dfrac{1}{150} + \dfrac{1}{100} \rightarrow EF = \dfrac{1}{\dfrac{1}{150} + \dfrac{1}{100}} = 60$.

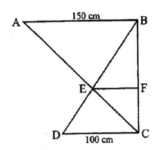

8. Solution: 32.6.

The length of the chord AB is equal to $AB = 2AE = 2 \times \sqrt{90^2 - 45^2} \approx 2 \times 77.94 \approx 155.88$.

The length of the arc $AB = \dfrac{120^0 \times 2\pi \times 90}{360^0} = 188.49$.

The distance saved walking along chord AB instead of walking from A to B along the semicircular path $CABD$ is 188.49 − 155.88 ≈ 32.6.

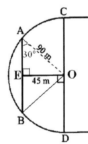

2000 Mathcounts National Sprint Round Solution

1. Solution: 91.

There are two pairs of prime numbers that add up to 20: (3, 17) and (7, 13). Since we want to find the greatest product, these two numbers should be as close as possible. $7 \times 13 = 91$ will be the greatest product (not $3 \times 17 = 51$).

Knowledge review: Prime numbers from 1 to 200:

	2	3	5	7	
11		13		17	19
		23			29
31				37	
41		43		47	
		53			59
61				67	
71		73			79
		83			89
				97	
101		103		107	109
		113			
				127	
131				137	139
					149
151				157	159
		163		167	169
		173			179
181					
191		193		197	199

2. Solution: 27.

Let Winslow's age be x and Abby's age be y.
According to the problem,
$x^2 + y = 209$

$x + y^2 = 183$.
$x^2 + y - (x + y^2) = (x - y)(x + y - 1) = 26 = 1 \times 26 = 2 \times 13$.

$\begin{cases} x + y - 1 = 26 \\ x - y = 1 \end{cases} \Rightarrow x = 14$ and $y = 13$. This is the desired solution.

Note $\begin{matrix} x + y - 1 = 13 \\ x - y = 2 \end{matrix}$ or other combinations do not produce positive integer solutions.

The sum of Abby's age and Winslow's age is 27.

2000 Mathcounts National Sprint Round Solution

3. Solution: 1.
$0.\overline{09} = \dfrac{9}{99} = \dfrac{1}{11} = 11^{-1}$.
$x = 1$.

4. Solution: $\dfrac{9}{2}\sqrt{3}$.

Triangle ABC is an equilateral triangle. The volume of the cube is 27 cubic inches, so one edge is 3 inches. The length of AB is $3\sqrt{2}$.

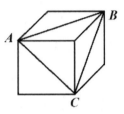

The area of triangle ABC is $A = \dfrac{1}{4}a^2\sqrt{3} = \dfrac{1}{4}(3\sqrt{2})^2 \times \sqrt{3} = \dfrac{9}{2}\sqrt{3}$.

5. Solution: 36.
There are a total of $8 \times 8 = 64$ digits. There are 8 one–digit numbers that can be created. This leaves 56 digits. These 56 digits can be used to create $56/2 = 28$ two-digit numbers, so the answer is $28 + 8 = 36$.

6. Solution: 8.
Let $a, b, c, d, e, f,$ and g represent the 7 integers from the smallest to the greatest. The median is 73, so d is 73.

a	b	c	d	e	f	g
			73	x	79	y

x or y or both need to be 79 so that the set has a mode of 79.
If only y is 79, then we have the set

a	b	c	d	e	f	g
70	71	72	73	7?	79	79

The difference between the maximum and minimum values is $79 - 70 = 9$.

If only x is 79, then we have the set

a	b	c	d	e	f	g
70	71	72	73	79	79	81

The difference is $81 - 70 = 11$.

If both x and y are 79, then we have

a	b	c	d	e	f	g
71	72	73	73	79	79	79

Or

71	71	73	73	79	79	79

2000 Mathcounts National Sprint Round Solution

The difference for both sets is 79 – 71 = 8.
The least possible difference is 8.

7. Solution: 34.
We can treat the third term as the first term, the 9th term as the 7th term, and the 13th term as the 11th term. All arithmetic sequences follow the following property:

$a_n = a_1 + (n-1)d$ or $20 = -1 + (7-1)d$

$d = \dfrac{21}{6} = \dfrac{7}{2}$ and $a_{11} = -1 + (11-1) \times \dfrac{7}{2} = 34$.

8. Solution: 9.
This question is the same as finding the solution for:
$x^2 + 2x - 19 < 0$ or $(x+1)^2 < 20$ or $-\sqrt{20} - 1 < x < \sqrt{20} - 1$.
Note $\sqrt{20} = 2\sqrt{5} \approx 4.4$, so the integer values of x are in the range $-6 < x < 4$. This gives a total of 9 values including –5, –4, –3, –2, –1, 0, 1, 2, 3.

9. Solution: 32.
Factor 876876:
$876876 = 876 \times 1001 = 4 \times 219 \times 13 \times 11 \times 7 = 2^2 \times 3 \times 73 \times 13 \times 11 \times 7$
There are $m = 3 \times 2 \times 2 \times 2 \times 2 \times 2 = 96$ positive integer factors of 876876.
Factor 678678:
$678678 = 678 \times 1001 = 2 \times 339 \times 13 \times 11 \times 7 = 2 \times 3 \times 113 \times 13 \times 11 \times 7$
There are $n = 2 \times 2 \times 2 \times 2 \times 2 \times 2 = 26 = 64$ positive integer factor of 678678.
$m - n = 96 - 64 = 32$.

10. Solution: 19.

	24	1	8	15
23		7	14	16
4	6	13		
10	12	n	21	3
		25		9

The sum from 1 to 25 is equal to $1 + 2 + 3 + \ldots + 25 = 325$.
Because the sum of the numbers in any row, any column, and any diagonal is the same, the sum of the numbers in any row, column, or diagonal is equal to $325/5 = 65$.
Looking at the 4th row, we have $10 + 12 + n + 21 + 3 = 65$, $n = 19$.

11. Solution: 755.
There are 10 palindromic numbers between 100 and 200.
    101   ~~111~~   ~~121~~   131   ~~141~~   151   ~~161~~   ~~171~~   181   191
However, only 5 of them are prime. The sum of all five is equal to $101 + 131 + 151 + 181 + 191 = 755$.

2000 Mathcounts National Sprint Round Solution

12. Solution:
List the possible outcomes:
```
615   514   413   312   211
624   523   422   321
633   532   431
642   541
651
```
The probability that at least one 3 is rolled is 7/15.

13. Solution: 9.
Let the number be ab.
$5(10a + b) = 6(10b + a)$
$\Rightarrow 50a + 5b = 60b + 6a$
$\Rightarrow 44a - 55b = 0$
$\Rightarrow 4a = 5b$.
Since 4 and 5 are relatively prime, $a = 5$ and $b = 4$. The sum of the digit of the number is 9.

14. Solution: $\frac{7}{10}$.

Method 1:

The number of ways to choose three balls from five is $\binom{5}{3} = 10$.

If we choose the ball numbered 1 as the first ball and the ball numbered 2 as the second ball (2 is the median), then there are three ways to choose the third ball (balls numbered 3, 4, or 5).

The probability that the median of the values on the three balls is 2 is $\frac{3}{10}$.

The probability that the median of the values on the three balls is greater than 2 is then: $1 - \frac{3}{10} = \frac{7}{10}$.

Method 2:
We just list the arrangements out:
```
1  2  3        1  2  4        1  2  5
1  3  4        1  3  5        1  4  5
2  3  4        2  3  5        2  4  5
3  4  5
```
Of the 10 total arrangements, 7 have a median greater than 2. The desired solution is $\frac{7}{10}$.

2000 Mathcounts National Sprint Round Solution

15. Solution: 72.
Draw $BE \perp AB$, then $\angle B = 60°$ and $\angle C = 30°$, forming a 30 – 60 – 90 triangle. So $BC = 18 = AB$. The perimeter of the rhombus equals $18 \times 4 = 72$.

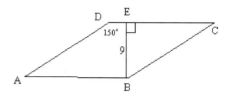

16. Solution: 32.
$$\frac{100!}{8^n} = \frac{100!}{2^{3n}}.$$
We can figure out how many 2's evenly divide 100!, and then divide the result by 3 to find how many 8's evenly divide 100!.
$$\left\lfloor \frac{100}{2} \right\rfloor + \left\lfloor \frac{100}{2^2} \right\rfloor + \left\lfloor \frac{100}{2^3} \right\rfloor + \left\lfloor \frac{100}{2^4} \right\rfloor + \left\lfloor \frac{100}{2^5} \right\rfloor + \left\lfloor \frac{100}{2^6} \right\rfloor = 50 + 25 + 12 + 5 + 3 + 1 = 96.$$

$3n = 96$, $n = 32$.

17. Solution: 252

Let $AC = x$ and $BC = y$.
We know that $MO = 12.5$ and $MB = 12.5 \times 2 = 25$.
$AB = 50$, so by the Pythagorean Theorem,
$$x^2 + y^2 = 50^2 \qquad (1)$$
The perimeter equals 112, so
$$x + y + 50 = 112 \qquad (2)$$
From (2), we get: $x + y = 62$ or $(x+y)^2 = 62^2$
Or $x^2 + 2xy + y^2 = 62^2 \qquad (3)$
(3) – (1) gives:
$2xy = 62^2 - 50^2$
$$\frac{xy}{2} = \frac{(60-50)(60+50)}{4} = \frac{12 \times 112}{4} = 336.$$
$S_{\triangle ANM} = \frac{1}{4} S_{\triangle ABC}$, so $S_{BCNM} = \frac{3}{4} S_{\triangle ABC} = \frac{3}{4} \times 336 = 252$.

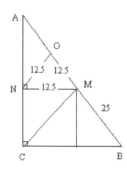

18. Solution: $\frac{17}{32}$.

2000 Mathcounts National Sprint Round Solution

Below is a list of all the arrangements satisfying the Triangle Inequality.

1	2	2		3
1	3	3		3
1	4	4		3
2	2	3		3
2	4	4		3
3	3	4		3
3	4	4		3
1	1	1		1
2	2	2		1
3	3	3		1
4	4	4		1
2	3	4		6

Total favorable outcomes = 24 + 4 + 6 = 34.

$$p = \frac{34}{4 \times 4 \times 4} = \frac{34}{64} = \frac{17}{32}.$$

19. Solution: 56.

Method 1:

Let t_1, t_2, t_3, and t_4 be the time in the specific section. The numbers are the corresponding speeds. The distance-rate formula says $d = rt$.

$$8t_1 = 8t_4$$
$$5t_2 = 20t_3 \quad (1)$$

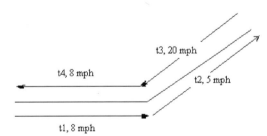

$$t_1 = t_4$$
$$t_2 = 4t_3 \quad (2)$$

$$t_1 + t_2 + t_3 + t_4 = 7 \quad (3)$$
$$2t_1 + 5t_3 = 7 \quad (4)$$

$$8t_1 + 5t_2 + 20t_3 + 8t_4 = 2d \quad (5)$$
$$8t_1 + 5t_2 = 20t_3 + 8t_4 = d \quad (6)$$
$$8t_1 + 20t_3 = d \quad (7)$$

$4 \times (4)$:
$$4(2t_1 + 5t_3) = 28 \quad \text{i.e. } 8t_1 + 20t_3 = 28$$

2000 Mathcounts National Sprint Round Solution

We know that $8t_1 + 20t_3 = d$, so d = 28. 2d will be 56.

Method 2:
Let D_1, D_2 be the distance traveled in the specific section. The numbers are the corresponding speeds.

$$V = \frac{D}{t}$$

$$= \frac{2(D_1 + D_2)}{\frac{D_1}{8} + \frac{D_2}{5} + \frac{D_2}{20} + \frac{D_1}{8}}$$

$$= \frac{2(D_1 + D_2)}{\frac{5D_1 + 8D_2 + 2D_2 + 5D_1}{40}}$$

$$= \frac{80(D_1 + D_2)}{10(D_1 + D_2)} = 8$$

$D = V \times t = 8 \times 7 = 56.$

Note: This is the general way to solve these kinds of problems.

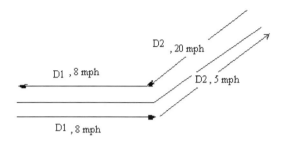

Method 3:
Let the average speed of v_2 and v_3 be v_{23}. Then

$$v_{23} = \frac{1 \times 2}{\frac{1}{5} + \frac{1}{20}} = 8.$$

Since $v_1 = v_{23} = v_4 = 8$, the total average speed is also 8. Since the total time is 7, the total distance is $7 \times 8 = 56$.

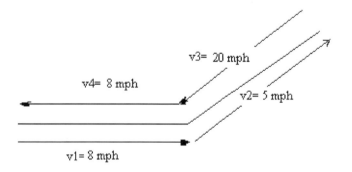

20. Solution: $\frac{64}{125}$.

The probability of drawing a marble that is not red is $1 - 1/5 = 4/5$.
Drawing three marbles with replacement, the probability that none of the marbles drawn will be red will be

$$p = \frac{4}{5} \times \frac{4}{5} \times \frac{4}{5} = \frac{64}{125}.$$

2000 Mathcounts National Sprint Round Solution

21. Solution: 91.
Method 1: Count directly:
There are 91 ways.

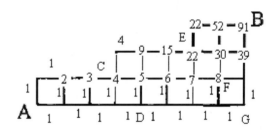

Method 2: Here is a more systematic way where we go through casework:
The paths must go through the points C, D, and E, F, and G.

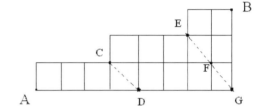

A to C to E to B: $\binom{4}{1} \times \binom{4}{1} \times \binom{3}{1} = 48$ ways

A to C to F to B: $\binom{4}{1} \times 1 \times \binom{3}{1} = 12$ ways

A to D to E to B: $1 \times \binom{4}{2} \times \binom{3}{1} = 18$ ways

A to D to F to B: $1 \times \binom{4}{2} \times \binom{3}{1} = 12$ ways

A to G to B: 1 way

Total ways $= 48 + 12 + 18 + 12 + 1 = 91$.

22. Solution: 5050.
$(100-99)(100+99) + (99-98)(99+98) + ... + (2-1)(2+1) = 100 + 99 + ... + 1$
$= 5050$.

23. Solution: 722.
Since the three numbers have an odd number of divisors, they must each be square numbers and less than 1000.
$n_1 = 2^4$; $n_2 = 3^4$ $n_3 = 4^4 (= 2^8$ having 8 factors and not counted); $n_4 = 5^4$.
The sum of the three numbers is $16 + 81 + 625 = 722$.

24. Solution: 240.
Note that the jobs are different and the kids are also different.

126

2000 Mathcounts National Sprint Round Solution

Since each kid will have at least one job, we have the following way to distribute the jobs:

    2,   1,   1,   1

One kid gets 2 jobs and the others each get one.

This gives us $\binom{5}{2} \times \binom{3}{1} \times \binom{2}{1} \times \binom{1}{1}$ ways.

Since kinds are different, we have $\dfrac{4!}{3!}$ to arrange them.

The answer is then $\binom{5}{2} \times \binom{3}{1} \times \binom{2}{1} \times \binom{1}{1} \times \dfrac{4!}{3!} = 240$.

25. Solution: 3.

Let $\sqrt{6 + \sqrt{6 + \sqrt{6 + \sqrt{6 + \ldots}}}} = x$

Square both sides to get $6 + \sqrt{6 + \sqrt{6 + \sqrt{6 + \sqrt{6 + \ldots}}}} = x^2$

or $6 + x = x^2$ or $x^2 - x - 6 = 0$.

Solve for x using the quadratic formula, $x = \dfrac{1 \pm \sqrt{1 + 24}}{2} = \dfrac{1 + 5}{2} = 3$.

26. Solution: 360.

Let the width be x and length be y.

The diagonal is 41 and the perimeter is 98, so

$x^2 + y^2 = 41^2$

$2(x + y) = 98 \to x + y = 49$.

Square both sides to get: $x^2 + 2xy + y^2 = 49^2$.

We know that $x^2 + y^2 = 41^2$, so $2xy = 49^2 - 41^2 = (49 - 41)(49 + 41) = 8 \times 90$.

$xy = 360$.

27. Solution: 14.

If we want find the least sum of the set, we need to factor out the number and let the factors be as close as possible to each other.

$144 = 12^2 = (2 \times 2 \times 3)^2 = 2 \times 2 \times 2 \times 2 \times 3 \times 3$.

The least sum will be $2 + 2 + 2 + 2 + 3 + 3 = 14$.

2000 Mathcounts National Sprint Round Solution

28. Solution: 8100.

The total number of ways to choose two different subcommittees with 2 boys and 2 girls is $\binom{6}{2}\binom{6}{2}\binom{4}{2}\binom{4}{2} = 15^2 \times 6^2 = (15 \times 6)^2 = 90^2 = 8100$.

29. Solution: 73.

Since there are a total of 40 pages, page # 1 and # 40 are on the same sheet, as well as #39 and # 2. In this newspaper, the two numbers on the same side of the sheet always sum to 41. Since page # 9 is missing, so the other number on the same side of the sheet is 32. We know that the sum of the other two numbers is 41. So the sum of the three missing page numbers is $32 + 41 = 73$.

30. Solution: 4.

We start from right hand side to makes the problem easier to solve:

$$\frac{3}{8} = \frac{1}{\frac{8}{3}} = \frac{1}{2 + \frac{2}{3}} = \frac{1}{2 + \frac{1}{\frac{3}{2}}} = \frac{1}{2 + \frac{1}{1 + \frac{1}{2}}}.$$

We see that $a = 2$, $b = 1$ and $c = 2$. The product will be 4.

2000 Mathcounts National Target Round Solution

1. Solution: 640.
Let the two positive integers be m and n. We want to find the value of mn.
$(m + n)^2 = 56^2$ (1)
$\dfrac{m}{n} + \dfrac{n}{m} = 2.9 = \dfrac{29}{10}$ (2)

From (1), we have: $m^2 + 2mn + n^2 = 56^2$ (3)

From (2), we have: $\dfrac{m^2+n^2}{mn} = \dfrac{29}{10}$ (4)

Substituting (3) into (4), we get $\dfrac{56^2-2mn}{mn} = \dfrac{29}{10} \Rightarrow \dfrac{56^2}{mn} - 2 = \dfrac{29}{10} \Rightarrow \dfrac{56^2}{mn} = \dfrac{29}{10} + 2 = \dfrac{49}{10}$.

By cross-multiplying, we get $mn = \dfrac{56^2 \times 10}{49} = \dfrac{7^2 \times 8^2 \times 10}{7^2} = 640$.

2. Solution: 1008.
If the algae doubles in 3 days, then in 6 days it is multiplied by 2^2. In 9 days it is multiplied by 2^3. The model describing the growth of the cells is: $G = k \times 2^{\frac{d}{3}}$ where G is the number of the cells, d is the number of days, and k is a constant (the beginning population of 100 in this case).
At the end of 10 days, the number of algae cells per milliliter can be expected to be
$G = k \times 2^{\frac{d}{3}} = 100 \times 2^{\frac{10}{3}} = 1007.9 = 1008$.

3. Solution: 25.
Megan travels x miles per minute on a bike and y miles per minute on feet. Let the distance from school to home be d miles.
The round-trip travel time, where she traveled both by bicycle and by foot, took Megan 35 minutes. From the distance-speed formula,
$\dfrac{d}{x} + \dfrac{d}{y} = 35$ (1)

The round-trip travel time by just bicycle is 30 minutes less than the round-trip travel time by walking, so
$\dfrac{2d}{x} - \dfrac{2d}{y} = 30$ (2)

We want to find out the number of minutes it takes for Megan to walk one way, $\dfrac{d}{y}$.

Multiply (1) by 2, we get:

2000 Mathcounts National Target Round Solution

$$\frac{2d}{x} + \frac{2d}{y} = 70 \qquad (3)$$

$(3) - (2) = \dfrac{d}{y} = 25$ minutes.

4. Solution: 3/7.
There are 36 total isosceles triangles that can be formed by three points (16, 8, 4, 4, and 4 in each of the following cases, respectively).

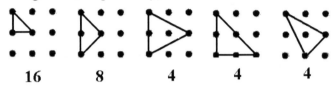

16   8   4   4   4

The total number of triangles that can be formed regardless of what type of triangle is formed is $\binom{9}{3} = 84$.

The probability of forming an isosceles triangle is $36/84 = 3/7$.

5. Solution: 98.
For every 30 digits, the following list is formed: 7418529630
After every third digit is picked to form a new number, the new number becomes:
    7418529630
    7418529630
    7418529630
    7418529630
    7418529630
    7418529630
    98

Every three rows (30 digits) above yields another new list: 1234567890
After the operation is completed once again, the new number becomes:
    1234567890
    1234567890
    98

After each third term is chosen again, the new list is:
3692589
One last process will give the resulting two-digit number: 98.

2000 Mathcounts National Target Round Solution

6. Solution: 8.6.
Method 1:
Annotate the figure as shown above. The Pythagorean theory tells us that:
$AB^2 + BC^2 = AC^2 \Rightarrow \quad 4^2 + 4^2 = AC^2 \Rightarrow \quad AC = 4\sqrt{2}$
The area of the smaller circle with a radius of $4\sqrt{2} - 4$ is
$\pi(4\sqrt{2} - 4)^2 = 8.6$.

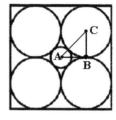

Method 2:
Annotate the figure as shown to the right.
$OC^2 = 8^2 + 8^2 = 2 \times 8^2 \quad \Rightarrow OC = 8\sqrt{2} \Rightarrow OO_1 = \frac{1}{2}OC = 4\sqrt{2}$.

The area of the smaller circle with a radius of $4\sqrt{2} - 4$ is
$\pi(4\sqrt{2} - 4)^2 = 8.6$.

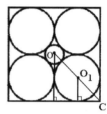

7. Solution: 10.
We have three cases:
Case I:
$x^2 - 5x + 5 = 1 \quad \Rightarrow \quad x^2 - 5x + 4 = 0$
$(x-1)(x-4) = 0$
$x = 1$ or $x = 4$.

Case II:
$x^2 - 7x + 12 = 0$ and $x^2 - 5x + 5 \neq 0$
$(x-3)(x-4) = 0 \quad \Rightarrow \quad x = 3$ or $x = 4$.
When $x = 3$, $x^2 - 5x + 5 = 9 - 15 + 5 = -1 \neq 0$. So $x = 3$ is a solution.
When $x = 4$, $x^2 - 5x + 5 = 16 - 20 + 5 = 1 \neq 0$. So $x = 4$ is also a solution.

Case III:
$x^2 - 5x + 5 = -1$ and $x^2 - 7x + 12$ is even.
$(x-2)(x-3) = 0 \quad \Rightarrow \quad x = 2$ or $x = 3$.
When $x = 2$, $x^2 - 7x + 12 = 4 - 14 + 12 = 2$, which is even. So $x = 2$ is a solution.
When $x = 3$, $x^2 - 7x + 12 = 9 - 21 + 12 = 0$, which is even. So $x = 3$ is a solution.
x can be 1, 2, 3, or 4. The sum of all values of x is 10.

8. Solution: 9.
Let the number of total marbles be x and the number of blue marbles be y.

2000 Mathcounts National Target Round Solution

The probability that two randomly selected marbles are both blue is 1/6. So,

$$\frac{\binom{y}{2}}{\binom{x}{2}} = \frac{1}{6} \quad \Rightarrow \quad \frac{y(y-1)}{x(x-1)} = \frac{1}{6} \quad (1)$$

The probability that three randomly selected marbles are all blue is 1/21. So,

$$\frac{\binom{y}{3}}{\binom{x}{3}} = \frac{1}{21} \quad \Rightarrow \quad \frac{y(y-1)(y-2)}{x(x-1)(x-2)} = \frac{1}{21} \quad (2)$$

Substituting (1) into (2):

$$\frac{y-2}{x-2} = \frac{2}{7} \quad \Rightarrow \quad 2x+10 = 7y \quad \Rightarrow \quad 2x+3 \equiv 0 \mod 7 \quad \Rightarrow \quad x \equiv 2 \mod 7$$

The smallest value for x and the fewest number of marbles that must have been in the bag before any were drawn is 9.

ATTACHMENT

Problems for 11 Sprint and 11 Target Tests

Note:

The problems attached are for your reference only. To avoid possible copyright issues, we have changed the *wording*, but not the *substance*, of the problems. Please refer to Mathcounts.org for original test problems if you have any question.

Test 1. Sprint Round Problems

1. What is the coefficient of the a^2b^2 term in the product of $(a+b)^2(a-b)^2$.

2. A circle is circumscribed about a regular hexagon. What is the ratio of the length of a side of the regular hexagon to the length of any diagonal which is not a diameter? Express your answer in the form $a:b$.

3. The original price of a coat was marked up 50%. The price was later reduced by 20% and finally the price was reduced an additional 10% and the coat was sold for $108 at a close-out sale. What is the original price paid for the coat by the shop owner?

4. The digits 1, 3, 5, or 7 are used to form the three-digit numbers. Each three-digit number is recorded on slips of paper and placed in a container. We pick up a slip of paper at random from the container. Find the probability that it contains the number 111.

5. Given a positive fraction. We multiply this fraction by $\dfrac{11}{60}$ to get a perfect integer cube greater than 1. Find the smallest such positive fraction

6. Given the set of numbers $\{a, b, c, d\}$, find $(b\nabla(a\nabla d))\nabla(b\nabla c)$ if the operation defined as follows:

∇	a	b	c	d
a	a	b	c	d
b	b	d	a	c
c	c	a	d	b
d	d	c	b	a

7. The HM, harmonic mean of two numbers a and b is the reciprocal of the average of their reciprocals and can be expressed as $HM = \dfrac{2}{\dfrac{1}{a}+\dfrac{1}{b}}$. Find the harmonic mean of 5 and

7. Express the answer as a mixed number.

8. Find the sum of the first 21 terms of the arithmetic series: $3 + 13 + 23 + \ldots$

9. Solve the radical equation for n: $\sqrt{5n+4} = 13$

Test 1. Sprint Round Problems

10. Find the length of the hypotenuse of a right triangle. The two legs of the right triangle have lengths that are in a 5 : 12 ratio and the perimeter of the triangle is 105. The answer should be expressed as a decimal number.

11. The year 1936 was a perfect square ($1936 = 44^2$). What is the absolute value of the difference between the next two years that were perfect squares?

12. Find the greatest prime factor of the least common multiple of 21, 24, and 60

13. To the nearest percent, find the percent of increase in the area of a circle if the diameter is increased by 25%.

14. Solve the following equation for x: $4[3(n-1)] + 5(n-1) - 7(n-1) = x(n-1)$.

15. We choose one element in the set below at random.
$\{16 - 2(8), 2(3)^2 - 17, 6 + 2(4) - 13, \frac{24}{3}(8), 4(3)^2 - 35\}$

Find the probability, expressed as a fraction, that its value will be 1.

16. We have several bags. Each bag contains 1000 of colored candies (red, brown, orange, green, and yellow). The candies are mixed well so that the colors are in the same proportion in all the bags. We examine one bag and a count of the different colors is summarized:

Color	Number
Red	||||| ||
Brown	||||| ||||
Orange	|||
Green	||||| |||
Yellow	||||| ||||| |||

We like to know how many yellow ones in two bags.

17. Find the total number of students voted in a school election based on the following data:

candidate A got $33\frac{1}{3}\%$ of the votes cast,

B got $\frac{9}{20}$ of the votes,

Test 1. Sprint Round Problems

C got $\frac{2}{15}$ of the votes, and
the only other candidate, D, got the remaining 75 votes.

18. We know that a typist produces four typed pages for every five handwritten pages and can type 14 pages per hour. Find the number of hours will it take him to type 105 handwritten pages.

19. We are given that the values of x and y shown below have a quadratic relationship.

x	2	3	4	5	10
y	7	17	31	49	199

Find the value of y if x = 14.

20. The number 21358tn is a seven-digit number. "t" is the tens digit and "n" is the units digit. Find the value of $\frac{n}{t}$ if 21358tn is divisible by 99.

21. We are given the following pattern:
$1 \times 9 + 2 =$ ———
$12 \times 9 + 3 =$ ———
$123 \times 9 + 4 =$ ———
Find the result of the calculation in the eighth line of the pattern if the same pattern is continued.

22. A company's sales changed as follows:
Increased $33\frac{1}{3}$% in 1986,
Decreased by 30% in 1987,
Decreased by 25% in 1988, and
Increased by 20% in 1989.
Total sales in 1989 were what percent of the sales at the beginning of 1986?

23. We select a three-digit number at random from all three-digit numbers, 100 through 999. We like that number to be a square number. Find the probability that number is a square number. The answer should be expressed as a fraction.

24. Solve the exponent equation for x: $\frac{3^{x^2}}{3^{3x}} = \frac{1}{9}$

Test 1. Sprint Round Problems

25. p is the least common multiple and q is the greatest common factor of 36 and 54. What will be the value for $\dfrac{p-q}{10}$?

26. Simplify the following expression. The answer should be expressed as a mixed number:

$$\cfrac{1}{1+\cfrac{1}{2+\cfrac{1}{3+\cfrac{1}{4+\cfrac{1}{5+\cfrac{1}{6}}}}}}$$

27. We are given rectangle $QRST$ in a rectangular coordinate system with $Q(-2,4)$ and $R(2,-4)$. The diagonal QS has a length of $2\sqrt{65}$. What is the area of the rectangle?

28. A father gave all of his money to his three daughters. To the first he gave half the money plus one-half dollar. To the second he gave half of what was left plus one-half dollar. To the third, he gave half of what was left plus one-half dollar. The second daughter want to buy a T-shirt of $6.25. How much money, in dollars, does she still need?

29. There are ten distinct points in a plane with no three of the points are collinear. Find the maximum number of distinct lines that can be drawn if these points are connected.

30. What is the sum of the value(s) of x that satisfy the given radical equation: $6\sqrt{(x-1)(x-2)(x-3)} + 6 = 6$.

Test 1. Target Round Problems

1. Find the number of disks Amy has under the following conditions:
She has fewer than 100 computer disks.
When she stacks them by elevens, ten are left over.
When she stacks them by tens, seven are left over
when she stacks them by sixes, three are left over

2. What is the value of m, expressed as an improper fraction, such that this relation is not a function. $\{(-2m + 1, -4), (-6m + 8, 0)\}$.

3. A standard dice has its faces numbered 1, 2, 3, 4, 5, and 6. A second dice has its faces numbered 2, 4, 6, 8, 10, and 12. What is the probability, expressed as a common fraction, to roll a sum of 8 when they are rolled?

4. The perimeter of a square is 16 inches greater than the perimeter of another square. If the area of the smaller square is 48 square inches less than the area of the larger, what is the sum, in inches, of the lengths of four diagonals of both squares.

5. Solve the inequality for integer values of x: $(x - 3)(x + 1)(x - 5) < 0$.

6. A golden rectangle is a rectangle such that the ratio of its width to length is the same as the ratio of its length to its width plus its length. If the width of a golden rectangle is one inch, find its length in inches.

7. As shown in the figure, three concentric circles have radii of 1, 3, and 6. If a point is randomly selected from the interior of the largest circle, find the probability, expressed as a common fraction, that it is in the region bounded by the two smaller circles.

8. m is the maximum number of regions within a circle that can be formed by four distinct lines intersecting the interior of the circle and n is the minimum number. What is $m + n$?

Test 2. Sprint Round Problems

1. What is the value of b^a if $2^a = 32$ and $a^b = 125$?

2. What is the greatest whole number that will satisfy this following inequality?
$4x - 3 < 2 - x$.

3. A cylindrical beaker is 8 cm high and has a radius of 3 cm. Find the number of such beakers of water needed to fill a spherical tank of radius 6 cm?

4. Solve the radical equation for n: $\sqrt{1 + \sqrt{2 + \sqrt{n}}} = 2$

5. The mean height of the five tallest buildings in Los Angeles in 1985 is 733 feet. The tallest of the five buildings is 858 feet high, and the shortest is 625 feet. If a new building were constructed with a height of 885 feet, by how many feet would it increase the mean height of the five tallest buildings in the city?

6. What is the geometric mean of $6\frac{1}{4}$ and 100?

7. n and m are whole numbers with $39 < n < 81$, and $19 < m < 41$. Find the greatest value for $\dfrac{n}{m} + \dfrac{m}{n}$? Express your answer as a mixed number.

8. Find the value of $m + n$ from the pattern below:
$1^3 = 1^2 - 0^2$
$2^3 = 3^2 - 1^2$
$3^3 = 6^2 - 3^2$
.
.
.
$6^3 = n^2 - m^2$

9. Find the difference between the largest and smallest prime factors of 15,015?

10. Points A and B are on the graph of $y = -\dfrac{1}{2}x^2$ such that triangle ABO is equilateral. What is the length of one side of triangle ABO?

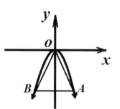

11. A phonograph record makes $33\frac{1}{3}$ revolutions per minute. Find

Test 2. Sprint Round Problems

the number of revolutions it will make in playing a record 3 minutes and 36 seconds long.

12. Compact discs cost $10.79 each, $17.75 for 2, and $33.25 for 4. Find the maximum number of discs that can be purchased with $130.

13. A tank was 26% full of water at the beginning. 700 gallons of water are added and the tank is 40% full now. Find the volume of the tank in gallons.

14. What is the value of n in the equation $\dfrac{1^3 + 2^3 + 3^3 + \ldots + n^3}{1 + 2 + 3 + \ldots + n} = 36$?

15. Car A left a city at 2:00 PM and traveled at an average speed of 40 miles per hour. Car B left at 4:00 PM, traveled the same route and overtook the first car at 9:00PM. Find the average speed in miles per hour of car B.

16. Find the units digit of the sum of all the integers from 100 to 202 inclusive.

17. In a class, the probability of earning an A is 0.7 times the probability of earning a B, and the probability of earning a C is 1.4 times the probability of earning a B. If the class has 31 students, find the number of students earning a B, assuming that all grades are A, B, or C.

18. The lines $y = -x - 1$, $x = 2$, and $y = \dfrac{1}{5}x + \dfrac{13}{5}$ intersect at three points. These points are exactly the vertices of a triangle. What is the equation of the circle passing through all three vertices?

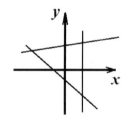

19. Lens A can increase the size of an image by 80% and lens B can increase the size by 50%. If these two lenses are used together, by what percent will the image be increased ?

20. Find the smallest composite number produced by $n^2 - n - 1$. n is a prime number.

21. The sum of the five 5 consecutive odd integers is 25 (1 + 3 + 5 + 7 + 9 = 25) and 25 is a square number. What is the median of the next larger set of 5 consecutive odd integers whose sum is a perfect square?

Test 2. Sprint Round Problems

22. The ratio of the length to width of a rectangle is 2:1. Find the area of the rectangle if the length of the diagonal is $5\sqrt{5}$.

23. The cubes with the edge lengths 1, 2, and 3, respectively, are stacked as shown in the figure. Find the length of the portion of segment $\overline{AB}$ that is contained in the center cube.

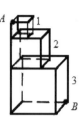

24. n is a positive integer divisible by 14 and having a square root between 25 and 25.3. What is the value of n?

25. 330 people are required to construct 30 km of railway track in 9 months. Find the number of months that are required for 275 people, working at the same rate, to construct 150 km of track.

26. Calculate: $\left(1\frac{1}{2}\right)^{-2} + \left(1\frac{1}{2}\right)^{-1} + \left(1\frac{1}{2}\right)^{0} + \left(1\frac{1}{2}\right)^{1} + \left(1\frac{1}{2}\right)^{2}$. Express your answer as a common fraction.

27. Solve the equation for x: $1 + \dfrac{1}{1 + \dfrac{1}{x} + \dfrac{1}{2x}} = \dfrac{7}{5}$.

28. A man is running through a train tunnel. When he is $\dfrac{2}{5}$ of the way through, he hears a train that is approaching the tunnel from behind him at a speed of 60 mph. Whether he runs ahead or runs back, he will reach an end of the tunnel at the same time the train reaches that end. Find the rate, in miles per hour, at which he is running. (Assume he runs at a constant rate.)

29. A fuel tanker weighs 2500 tons when 25% full and 3700 tons when 75% full. Find its weight in tons when empty.

30. As shown in the figure, point A of a rectangular piece of paper of width 8 inches is folded over so that it coincides with point C on the opposite side. Find the length in inches of fold l if $BC = 5$ inches.

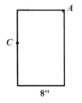

Test 2. Target Round Problems

1. What percent of all three-digit positive integers contains the digit 5 at least once?

2. We have a set of consecutive odd integers. The number of these odd integers is odd. The arithmetic mean of these odd integers is y. What is the sum of the smallest and largest of the integers? Express your answer in terms of y.

3. Find the 100th digit of the decimal representation of $\frac{1}{7}$.

4. Equilateral triangle ABC has the side length of 2 cm. $\overline{BC}$ is extended its own length to D, and E is the midpoint of $\overline{AB}$. $\overline{ED}$ meets $\overline{AC}$ at F. What is the area of the quadrilateral $BEFC$ in square centimeters in simplest radical form?

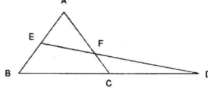

5. A train travels its own length in 3 seconds. It approaches a station 336 feet long. From the time the front of the train reaches the station, 10 seconds elapse. Find the length in feet of the train.

6. Find is the sum of the prime factors of the number represented by
$2^{12} - 2^{11} + 2^{10} - 2^9 + \ldots + 2^2 - 2^1$.

7. A driver's pocket contains 2 quarters, 2 dimes, and 2 nickels. When he approaches a toll booth. He randomly selects two coins from his pocket. Find the probability that the value of the two coins he selects will be at least enough to pay the 30-cent toll. Express your answer as a common fraction.

8. Octagon $ABCDEFGH$ is a regular octagon of side 12 cm. What is the area in square centimeters of trapezoid $BCDE$. Express your answer in simplest radical form.

Test 3. Sprint Round Problems

1. An estate was divided among three people. Andrea received 20% of the estate and her mother received 50% of what remained, leaving $20,000 for Andrea's uncle. Find the total value of the estate.

2. As shown in the figure, $ABCD$ is a square with $AB = 5$. $AE = AF = CG = CH$. The shaded region is five-ninths of the area of $ABCD$. What is the length of AF? Express your answer as a common fraction.

3. The sum of any three terms in a certain sequence of numbers is 3. The second term is 4 and the fourth term is -2. Find the 18th term in this sequence.

4. For how many ordered pairs of positive integers (x, y) does y exceed x least 2? $3 \leq y \leq 22$.

5. What is the smallest real value of x that satisfies the following equation?
$(x + 5)(x^2 - x - 11) = x + 5$.

6. Stacey can trim the shrubbery in six hours working alone. Her father can do it in five hours working alone. Find the number of hours they worked together to trim $\frac{11}{15}$ of the shrubbery.

7. How many distinguishable ways are there to arrange four identical red chips and two identical white chips a circle?

8. The quotient is 33 when the product of three consecutive positive integers is divided by their sum. Find the largest of the three integers.

9. $n* = n - 1b$ defines the operation "*". Find the value $10(3 *) - 5(4 *)$.

10. The die whose faces are shown in the figure is rolled and the numbers on the four lateral faces are added. Find the probability that the sum is a prime number. Express your answer as a common fraction.

11. Calculate $\frac{1}{2} + \frac{1}{2^2} + \frac{1}{2^3} + \cdots + \frac{1}{2^{10}}$. Express your answer as a common fraction.

12. Find the units digit of $2^{40} - 1$.

Test 3. Sprint Round Problems

13. Find the number of integer solutions to $f(x) < 3$ if $f(x) = |x-1|$.

14. Find the smallest possible integer value of n such that $m + n > 50$ and $m - n \leq 10$.

15. Daryl is two-thirds as old as he will be eight years before he is twice as old as he is now. How old is he now?

16. As shown in the figure, two congruent regular 20-sided polygons are placed side by side. What is the degree measure of $\angle ABC$?

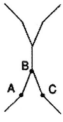

17. Find the volume, in terms of π, of the figure generated by the rotation of right triangle AOC, as shown in the figure, about the y-axis.

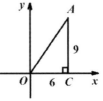

18. Find the value of $|a+b|$ if $7a^2 + 3a^2b + 14ab - 2ab^2 = 61$ and $7b^2 - 3a^2b + 2ab^2 = 2$.

19. As shown in the figure, the right circular cone has a height of 8 inches and the radius of the base is 6 inches. A one-inch thick slice, parallel to the base and two inches from the vertex, is removed. What is the volume, in cubic inches, of the slice. Express your answer as a common fraction in terms of π.

20. As shown in the figure, $BDEF$ is a rhombus with vertices on $\triangle ABC$. Find DE if $AB = 10$ and $BC = 15$.

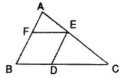

Test 3. Sprint Round Problems

21. The function defined by $f(x) = \dfrac{1}{x} - 2$. Find the real number that is not contained in the range of the function.

22. Find the 4,000th term of the following sequence: 1, 2, 2, 3, 3, 3, 4, 4, 4, 4, 5, 5, 5, 5, 5, 6 . . .

23. Find the number of zeros 50! ends when it is expressed in standard base ten notation.

24. What is the greatest number of bags that can be used to hold 190 marbles if each bag must contain at least one marble, but no two bags may contain the same number of marbles?

25. Digit d is randomly selected from the set {4, 5, 6, 7} with replacement. A digit e is then randomly selected. Find the probability that the two-digit number de is a multiple of 3. Express your answer as a common fraction.

26. The area of a triangle is 7.5 square units. Find the positive number x, if the vertices of the triangle have coordinates (−3, 1), (−2, −3), and (x, 0).

27. Two satellites circle the earth in the opposite direction and at the same altitude. Satellite A circles the earth in 48 hours. Satellite B passes satellite A every 16 hours. Find the number of hours it takes satellite B to circle the earth.

28. As shown in the figure, equilateral triangle $\triangle DCE$ is inside square $ABCD$. $FE = 1$. $FE // AD$. What is the length of DC? Express your answer in simplest radical form.

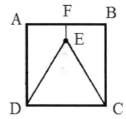

29. The 9-digit number 708, a6b, 8c9 is a multiple of 99, where a, b, and c are distinct digits. What is the value of $a + b + c$?

30. What is the number of positive integral divisors of 792?

Test 3. Target Round Problems

1. Find the number of zeros ended in the expression $\dfrac{50!}{19! \cdot 31!}$ when written in standard form.

2. Find the time when the minute and hour hands of a clock are perpendicular to each other the first time between 4:00 and 5:00. Express your answer to the nearest second in the form $\dfrac{\quad}{\text{hr}} : \dfrac{\quad}{\text{min}} : \dfrac{\quad}{\text{sec}}$.

3. Find the largest integral divisor of $2^{14} - 1$ that is less than $2^{14} - 1$.

4. As shown in the figure, a circle with a radius of one yard has within it an infinite sequence of concentric circles. The radius of each circle is one-half the radius of the next larger circle. Find the total area, in square yards, of the shaded region if the shading pattern continues infinitely. Express your answer as a common fraction in terms of π.

5. As shown in the figure, four points on the geoboard are selected at random. Find the probability that they will be vertices of a square. Express your answer as a common fraction.

6. As shown in the figure, a dart board has two scoring areas: 4 and 9. Find the highest score that cannot be attained if an unlimited number of darts is allowed.

7. As shown in the figure, each of the circles has a radius of 6, and $DE = 6$. What is the area of the shaded region? Express your answer to the nearest square unit. Use 3.14 for π.

8. Find the sum of all positive divisors of 770.

146

Test 4. Sprint Round Problems

1. Two more students are ahead of me in line than are behind me. Three times as many students are in line as the number of students who are behind me. Find the number of students ahead of me in line.

2. In a dinner party, Jim and John bought 8 dishes of food of equal value. 5 dishes were purchased by Jim and 3 by John. Jan decides to join them and agrees to pay $8, an equal $\frac{1}{3}$ of the cost of the meal. The $8 is to be split between Jim and John so everyone contributes the same. Find the number of dollars Jim will get.

3. Find the units digit of $(b^a)^2$. $a^b = 125$ and a and b are whole numbers less than 20.

4. Each of the fractions $\frac{1}{7}, \frac{2}{7}, \frac{3}{7}, \frac{4}{7}, \frac{5}{7}$, and $\frac{6}{7}$ is written as a repeating decimal. In one of the repeating decimals, the third and fourth digit after the decimal point form a two-digit number which is one-half of the number formed by the fifth and sixth digit. What is the fraction corresponding to this decimal?

5. Find the value of $(\frac{1}{3})^3$ if $\frac{1}{3} = 0.33333....$ Express your answer as a decimal rounded to the nearest thousandth.

6. The volume of a cube is 2,197 cubic centimeters. Find its total surface area in square centimeters.

7. Find the number of three-digit positive integers that do not contain a zero.

8. A bag contains six red marbles, eight yellow marbles, and seven blue marbles. Three marbles are drawn at random one by one without replacement from the bag.
Find the probability that two red marbles and one blue marble will be drawn in that order. Express your answer as a common fraction.

9. As shown in the figure, seven points are equally distributed on a circle. Find the number of non-congruent quadrilaterals that can be drawn with vertices chosen from among the seven points,

10. Find the equivalent value of $\sqrt{5 - 2\sqrt{6}}$ expressed in simplest radical form $\sqrt{a} - \sqrt{b}$, where a and b are positive integers.

Test 4. Sprint Round Problems

11. What is the product of all numbers of the form $((1-\frac{1}{n})^{-1}$? $2 \le n \le 15$.

12. What is the value of $f(8)$ if $f(2) = 1$? $f(n)$ is defined by $f(n+2) = \dfrac{n}{f(n)}$ for all positive integer n.

13. For $x \ne \{0, 1\}$, simplify $\dfrac{(1-\frac{1}{x})^{-1} + 1}{(1-\frac{1}{x})^{-1} - 1}$.

14. A right triangle has the vertices at (2, 3), (7, 8), and (−1, 16). Find the slope of the line containing the hypotenuse. Express your answer as a common fraction.

15. Find the smallest possible integer d greater than 1 such that the remainders will be the same when the three integers 618, 343, and 277 are divided by d.

16. As shown in the figure, all the triangles are equilateral. Find the ratio of the shaded area to the area of triangle ABC.

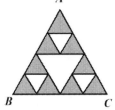

17. In an arithmetic sequence of five terms, the sum of the last three is 48 and the sum of all five terms 55. What is the sum of the first three terms?

18. Find the percent of the even perfect squares between 100 and 1000. Express your answer to nearest tenth of a percent.

19. Find the sum of $1^3 + 2^3 + 3^3 + \ldots + 20^3$.

20. Find the value of the product of x and y if $\left(\dfrac{1}{(x+y)}\right)\left(\dfrac{1}{x} + \dfrac{1}{x}\right) = \dfrac{1}{13}$.

21. Find the 700th digit to the right of the decimal point of the number 0.3456789101112…333. The number 0.3456789101112…333 is created by writing the numbers 3 to 333 in order after the decimal point.

148

Test 4. Sprint Round Problems

22. Find the number of digits in the expanded form of 2 to the 40th power.

23. What is the value of $\dfrac{1}{2}+\dfrac{1}{6}+\dfrac{1}{12}+\dfrac{1}{20}+\cdots+\dfrac{1}{9900}$? Express your answer as a common fraction.

24. Bottle A contains more Diet Coke than Bottle B. Now do the following:
   a. Pour from bottle A into B as much Diet Coke as B already contains.
   b. Pour from bottle B into A as much Diet Coke as A now contains.
   c. Pour from bottle A into B as much Diet Coke as B now contains.
Both bottles now have 64 ounces. How many more ounces were in A than in B at the beginning?

25. Seventy four hens lay 74 dozen eggs in 74 days. Thirty seven hens eat 37 kilograms of wheat in 37 days. Find the number of kilograms of wheat needed to produce 1 dozen eggs.

26. Alice drives at a constant speed. After a while, she passes a mile marker showing a two-digit number. One hour later, she passes a second marker with the same two digits in reverse order. In another hour she passes a third marker with the same two digits separated by a zero. Find the rate of Alice's car in miles per hour.

27. Three boys play 4 rounds of a game and end with a tie score of 80. A different player wins each of the final three rounds. When a player wins, he doubles his points, and the two losers each must subtract the amount the winner gains from their scores. Find the highest score at the end of round 1.

28. A small town has 100 men. Among them, 85 are married, 70 have a telephone, 75 own a car, and 80 own their own home. On this basis, find the smallest possible number of men who are married, have their own telephone, own their own car, and own their own home.

29. Find the remainder when 5 to the 999,999th power is divided by 7.

30. Auggie spent all of his money in 5 stores. In each store, he spent $1 more than one-half of what he had when he went in. How many dollars did Auggie have when he entered the first store?

Test 4. Target Round Problems

1. As shown in the figure, two squares are arranged next to each other. Find the shaded area in square centimeters. Express your answer as a decimal.

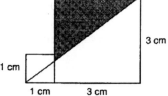

2. Eight cups of pure grape juice are mixed with 16 cups of water in a container. Two cups of the mixture are removed from the container and then two cups of water are added. What fractional part of the mixture is the grape juice?

3. At the end of the first week, a worm's length has increased by one-half of its original length. At the end of the second week, its length had increased by one-third from the previous week, the third week by one-fourth from the previous week, and so on. After n weeks the worm's length was 20 times as long as its original length. What is n?

4. The radius of sphere A is 9 inches. The volume of sphere B is twice the volume of sphere A. Find the diameter in inches of sphere B. Express your answer in simplest radical form.

5. Four points on the geoboard below are randomly selected. What is the probability the four points are the vertices of a square? Express your answer as a common fraction.

6. What is the value of $a + b + c + d$ in the following equation? a, b, c, and d are positive integers.

$$a + \cfrac{1}{b + \cfrac{1}{c + \cfrac{1}{d}}} = \frac{181}{42}$$

Test 4. Target Round Problems

7. Find the degree measure of angle *BAC* in triangle *ABC*, as shown in the figure. $AX = XY = YB = BC$. $\angle ABC = 120°$.

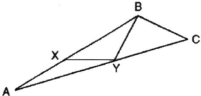

8. What is the 5-digit number for which all of the following are true:
a) The number's first two digits express a perfect square;
b) The number's middle digits is a perfect square;
c) The number's last two digits express a perfect square.
d) The number's square root is a prime palindrome;

Test 5. Sprint Round Problems

1. We have the following operation ★ on the set of numbers $\{x, y, z, w\}$ defined in the table:

★	x	y	z	w
x	x	y	z	w
y	y	w	x	z
z	z	x	w	y
w	w	z	y	x

Find the value of $(y ★ (x ★ (x ★ w))) ★ (y ★ z)$.

2. A board consists of three concentric circles of radii 2, 3, and 4, respectively. A dart is thrown randomly at the board and it hits inside one of the circles. Find the probability that the dart is in the interior of the circle of radius 3 but not in the interior of the circle of radius 2. Expressed the answer as a common fraction.

3. A right cylindrical can holds tightly three identical tennis balls so that the balls cannot move inside the can. The radius of each ball is 4 cm. What is the number of cubic centimeters in the volume of the space within the cylinder, not taken up by the three tennis balls. Express your answer in terms of π.

4. A window consists of a semicircular sheet of glass and a rectangular sheet of glass. The rectangular sheet of glass has dimensions of 4 feet by 3.5 feet. The semicircular sheet of glass is on the top of the rectangular sheet of glass with the side of 3.5 ft as the diameter. Find the number of feet of weather-stripping needed to go around the window. Express your answer to the nearest integer.

5. As shown in the figure, the angle B and angle C of a scalene triangle ABC are trisected. The trisectors meet at points P and Q, respectively. $\angle A = 30°$. What is the measure in degrees of $\angle BPC$.

Test 5. Sprint Round Problems

6. Positive integers 1 through 8 are divided into two groups A and B. The product of the positive integers in A is a. The product of the positive integers in B is b. The larger of a and b is written down. Find the smallest possible number that can be written down using this procedure.

7. Roses is sold for $20.00 per dozen, daisies for $5.00 per dozen, and chrysanthemums for $10.00 per dozen. Find the number of dollars to buy 9 roses, 6 daisies, and 18 chrysanthemums.

8. Find the value of $m + n$ so that $m > n$ and m is not a multiple of n. m and n are positive integers satisfying the equation $\dfrac{1}{m} + \dfrac{1}{n} = \dfrac{2}{15}$.

9. Find $a + b + c$ with the pattern below to express 100^2 in the form $a^2 + b^2 - c^2$.
$12^2 = 8^2 + 9^2 - 1^2$
$14^2 = 10^2 + 10^2 - 2^2$
$16^2 = 12^2 + 11^2 - 3^2$
$18^2 = 14^2 + 12^2 - 4^2$

10. The ratio of the length of a rectangle to its width is the same as that of the diagonal to the length. Find the length of the diagonal if the width is 2. Express the answer in the simplest radical form.

11. How much greater is x than its reciprocal if x satisfies $x^2 - 4x - 1 = 0$?

12. Find the difference between the largest and the smallest values of x satisfying the following system of inequalities. Express your answer as a mixed number.
$2x - 6 \leq 6$
$4x + 3 \geq 13$

13. a, b, and c are distinct odd integers between 2 and 20. How many different values can be expressed by $a + b + c$?

14. Solve the following equation for x: $\{3 + [2 + (1 + x^2)^2]^2\}^2 = 144$.

15. A Pythagorean triple can be expressed as $(x^2 - y^2)$, $2xy$, and $(x^2 + y^2)$. x and y are positive integers with $x > y > 0$. The chart below shows the Pythagorean triples formed by some values of x and y. What is the value of x which will yield the Pythagorean triple 12, 16, 20?

Test 5. Sprint Round Problems

x	y	$x^2 - y^2$	$2xy$	$x^2 + y^2$
2	1	3	4	5
3	1	8	6	10
4	1	15	8	17
5	1	24	10	26
?	?	12	16	20

16. As shown in the figure, is a "chalk" container for a cue stick in billiards. The cube has edges of length 2 cm. The hemispherical depression has a radius $\frac{1}{2}$ cm. Find the number of cubic centimeters in the volume of the remaining chalk in the cubical container. Express your answer in terms of π.

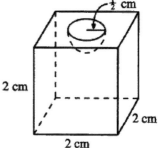

17. Solve the following radical equation for x: $\sqrt{3x+1} = 3x+1$.

18. Find the seventh term in the sequence 2, 3, 5, 9, ... The rule to form the sequence is $t_{n+1} = 2 \cdot t_n - 1$ with $t_1 = 2$.

19. Find the number of units in the length of one diagonal of a square described by the equation $|x+2| + |y-3| = 1$.

20. Find the minimum value of the function $y = x^2 - 6x + 5$.

21. Solve the following factorial equation for N: $\dfrac{7!\,8!\,9!}{7!+8!+9!} = \dfrac{8!\,N!}{9}$.

22. Find N, the number of sides of a polygon if N is twice the square root of the number of diagonals of the polygon.

23. The ratio of the areas of two squares is 3 : 1. What is the ratio of the perimeters of the larger square to the smaller square? Express your answer in the form x : 1 with x rounded to the nearest tenth.

Test 5. Sprint Round Problems

24. M people pay a total of $\$X$ to travel on a tour bus. How much more money, in dollars, will it cost for M plus N people to travel on the bus if these additional n people have to pay the same fare as the first M people while the original fare for M people is not changed? Express the answer in terms of N, M, and X.

25. Triangle ABC is a right triangle with $\angle C = 90°$. The length of the altitude from C to the side AB is 12 inches. Find the area of the triangle if the perimeter is 60 inches.

26. The pattern of Mr. Smith's account activities is as follows:
On the fifth of each month a $1.50 service charge is assessed regardless of the balance.
He makes a $10.00 withdrawal on the twentieth day of each month.
Find the balance of Mr. Smith's account on September 1 if he has an account balance of $97.00 on January 1.

27. A rectangular block with the dimensions of 30 cm, 16 cm, and 12 cm is made from cubes which are each 1 cm^3 in volume. The outside of the block is painted red and then separated into the original cubes. Find the percentage of the block with exactly two sides painted red. Express your answer to the nearest tenth.

28. 120 eight-inch square tiles are used to cover a floor entirely without overlapping. Find the number of two-inch square tiles needed to cover entirely the same floor.

29. What is the value of 9^{2x+2}? $3^{x+1} = 5$.

30. A house was sold for $73,780. The selling price represented 8.5% profit over the purchase price. Find the original purchase price in dollars of the house.

Test 5. Target Round Problems

1. If $n - 2d$ is divisible by 7, then $10n + d$ is divisible by 7. d is a digit and n is a positive integer. Given that the fifteen digit number 123, 456, 789, 101, 112 is 5 bigger than a multiple of 7, find the digit d for which the sixteen digit number 1,234,567,891,011,12d is a multiple of 7.

2. A group of math teachers agreed to split the luncheon bill equally. When the bill arrived, two of the teachers said that they did not bring their money. The others in the group agreed to make up the difference by each paying an extra $1.30. Find the number of teachers in the group ff the total bill was $78.00.

3. Line l_1 is represented by the equation $y = m_1 x + 10$ and line l_2 is represented by the equation $y = m_2 x + 9$. m_1 is randomly selected from $\{0!, (\frac{1}{2})^{-1}, \sqrt[3]{-1}\}$ and m_2 is randomly selected from $\{\frac{6!}{5!}, -\sqrt{\frac{1}{4}}, -1\}$. Find the probability that l_1 and l_2 are parallel.

4. $\frac{19}{20} < \frac{1}{k} + \frac{1}{n} + \frac{1}{m} < 1$, where k, n, and m are positive integers. Find the smallest possible value of $k + n + m$.

5. Find the value of $(1 - \frac{1}{6}) + (\frac{1}{2} - \frac{1}{7}) + (\frac{1}{3} - \frac{1}{8}) + \cdots + (\frac{1}{95} - \frac{1}{100})$. Express your answer as a decimal to the nearest tenth.

6. As shown in the figure, the side AB of triangle ABC is extended to D. The angle bisectors of $\angle BAC$ and $\angle CBD$ of triangle ABC meet at E (not shown in the figure). If the angle formed by these two bisectors is 50 degrees, what is the number of degrees in angle C of triangle ABC?

7. As shown in the figure, fifteen balls of diameter 2.25 inches are arranged to form the "triangle". Find the minimum length, in inches, of metal band required to enclose the balls. Express your answer in terms of π

Test 5. Target Round Problems

8. As shown in the figure, a farmer has a rectangular animal run for her cows, horses, and pigs. She wants each type of animal to have the same area. Find the largest number of square meters which can be enclosed if she has 60 meters of fence. Express your answer as a decimal.

Test 6. Sprint Round Problems

1. As shown in the figure, *BDEF* is a square. *AB* = *BC* = 1. What is the number of square units in the area of the regular octagon?

2. Find the number of zeros at the end of the whole-number representation of $\frac{20!}{10^4}$.

3. A solid composed of a 1″ cube stacked upon a 3″ cube which in turn is stacked upon a 5″ cube. The entire solid is to be painted. What is the number of square inches of the surface that will be painted?

4. Extra credit is awarded on quizzes to students with quiz grades that exceed the class mean. If 107 students take the same quiz, find the largest number of students who can be awarded extra credit.

5. The number of students in East Junior High math club increases from 75 (last year) to 99 (this year). The increase represents a growth of 25% for girls and 40% for boys. Find the number of girls in the math club last year.

6. A spherical balloon filled with water lands on a sidewalk, momentarily flattening to a hemisphere. Find the ratio of the radius of the spherical balloon to the radius of the hemisphere. Express your answer as a common fraction in simplest radical form.

7. To obtain 45 ounces of 24% acid solution, a 30% acid solution is mixed with 20% acid solution. Find the number of ounces of 20% acid solution needed.

8. The median is 30 and mean is 32 of the ordered numbers 18, 21, 24, *a*, 36, 37, and *b*.. What is the positive difference between *a* and *b*?

9. Equilateral triangles *A* has sides of length *x* and equilateral triangles *B* has sides of length 2*x*. Equilateral triangle *C* has the same area as the sum of the areas of the two original triangles. What is the number of units in the length of the side of the equilateral triangle *C*? Express your answer in terms of *x*.

Test 6. Sprint Round Problems

10. A box contains six straws of lengths 2 cm, 3 cm, 4 cm, 5 cm, 6 cm, and 7 cm. Three straws are drawn at random without replacement. What is the probability that these three straws will form a triangle when connected at their endpoints? Express the answer as a common fraction

11. Find the number of square units in the area of the region determined by the following system:
$$|x| + |y| \leq 4$$
$$y \leq 0$$

12. What is the product of all real numbers n which satisfy the following equation?
$$|n^2 - 9n + 20| = |16 - n^2|.$$

13. The perimeter of a rectangle is 4 units. Its width is $\frac{2}{3}$ of its length. Find the number of square units in the area of the rectangle. Express the answer as a common fraction.

14. Find the number of three-digit odd integers greater than 299.

15. A coin purse contains 30 coins whose value is $5. These coins are either nickels, dimes, and/or quarters. Find the number of possible different combinations of these coins.

16. Find the remainder when 9^{1995} is divided by 7.

17. As shown in the figure, a chord of the larger of two concentric circles is tangent to the smaller circle. The chord measures 18 inches. What is the number of square inches in the area of the shaded region? Express your answer in terms of π.

18. The sequence 7, a, —, —, —, 11 is formed such that each term after the second is the sum of the two preceding terms. What is the value of a?

19. As shown in the figure, both *RECT* and *LONG* are rectangles. Find the number of square units in the area of *LONG*.

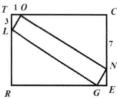

159

Test 6. Sprint Round Problems

20. As shown in the diagrams, figure 2 is obtained by dividing the shaded area in figure 1 into four congruent squares and the upper left square of the four is painted white. Find the fractional part of the tenth figure that will be shaded if the pattern continues. Express your answer as a common fraction in which the numerator and denominator are expressed in prime factored form using exponents.

1 2 3

21. Find f(4) if f is a function defined by $f(n) = f(n-1) + 2n$, for $n > 0$ with $f(0) = 0$.

22. A rectangular region with a perimeter of 30 cm is formed by some 1-cm square tiles. A square region can also be formed by the same number of tiles. Find the perimeter of the square region.

23. As shown in the figure, a medieval weapon consists of 4 arcs which are semicircles of radius 6 inches. Point X is the centroid of the weapon. Find the number of square inches in the area of the cross-section of the weapon.

24. What is the sum of a and b if $f(x)$ defined by $f(x) = a \cdot 2^{bx}$ contains the points (0, 3) and (1, 24)?

25. Four on/off switches are arranged in a row. Find the number of ways to set them so that no two adjacent switches are on.

26. The equation $c = t - 40$ shows the relationship between the rate at which crickets chirp and the temperature. c is the number of chirps per 15 seconds and t is the temperature in degrees Fahrenheit. Find number of degrees Fahrenheit in the temperature when a cricket chirps 500 times in 5 minutes.

27. The distance from your home to the beach is 260 miles. Your average speed is 65 mph to the beach and 40 mph on the return trip. Find the mean speed for the entire trip. Express your answer in miles per hour to the nearest whole number.

28. Four-digit positive integers are formed with the digits 2, 4, 5, 6, and 7 without repetition. Find the number of such positive integers divisible by four.

29. The figure shows the first six rows of Pascal's triangle, beginning with row zero.

Test 6. Sprint Round Problems

Row 4 consists of only even numbers except for the '1' at each end. Row 2 exhibits the same property. Find the number of rows among the first 20 rows with this property.

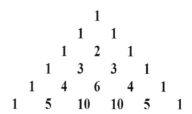

30. Solve for k: $\dfrac{k(n-2)!}{(n+1)!} = \dfrac{(n-1)!}{(n+2)!}$. Express the answer as a common fraction in terms of n, where n is an integer greater than 1.

Test 6. Target Round Problems

1. What is the area of the region formed by the following inequalities?
$$x + y \geq 2$$
$$x \geq 0$$
$$y \geq 0$$
$$y \leq 3$$
$$x \leq 5$$

2. As shown in the figure, a dart board has two scoring areas: 7 and 15. Find the largest finite score that cannot be attained if an unlimited number of darts is allowed.

3. The whole numbers are listed as shown in the figure. If the pattern continues, find the number of the row in which the number 120,000 is listed.

Row 1					0				
Row 2				1	2	3			
Row 3			8	7	6	5	4		
Row 4		9	10	11	12	13	14	15	
Row 5	24	23	22	21	20	19	18	17	16

4. The horizontally and vertically adjacent points in this square grid are 1 cm apart. What is the number of centimeters in the perimeter of the polygon?
Express your answer as a decimal to the nearest hundredth.

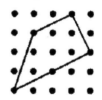

5. As shown in the figure, all angles are right angles. Find the total number of rectangles in the diagram.

Test 6. Target Round Problems

6. What is the value of $f(1)$ if the function $f(x)$ is defined as follows.
$$f(x) = \begin{cases} x - 2 & \text{for } x > 5, \\ x - f(f(x+3)) & \text{for } x \leq 5. \end{cases}$$

7. Twenty posts are equally spaced around the circumference of a circular corral. Each post contributes 6 inches to the circumference and the fencing between adjacent posts contributes 8 feet to the circumference. Find the number of square feet in the area of the corral. Express your answer to the nearest integer.

8. Three vertices of a triangle are $A(-2, 2)$, $B(-8, 2)$, and $C(-8, -1)$. Find the coordinates of the reflection of A about the line $y = 2x + 1$. Express the coordinates of the reflection of A as an ordered pair.

Test 7. Sprint Round Problems

1. There are three positive integers and the sum of them is 220. If they are listed in order from the smallest to the largest, the first two are consecutive integers and the last two are consecutive odd integers. Find the product of the smallest and largest.

2. Wanda's four pet pot-bellied piglets were weighed in pairs. Oinker and Squeaker weighed 110 pounds, Squeaker and Curly weighed 103 pounds, and Curly and Porker totaled 108 pounds. Find the number of pounds Oinker and Porker.

3. As shown in the figure, O is the center of the circle. $\angle RIP = 36°$. $OR = 10$ cm. What is the number of centimeters in the length of $\overarc{RP}$? Express your answer in terms of π.

4. Find the number of integral solutions for x in the inequality $\frac{1}{2} \le \frac{x}{8} \le \frac{7}{9}$.

5. An ID number consists of a four-digit number, such as 0228. If an ID number is selected at random, find the probability that no two of its digits are the same. Express your answer as a decimal to the nearest thousandths.

6. $ABCD$ is a square. A point E is chosen randomly inside the square. What is the probability that $\triangle ABE$ is obtuse? Express your answer as a decimal to the nearest hundredth.

7. Find the number of positive integers n satisfy the inequality $3 < \sqrt[n]{100} < 5$.

8. Charlie's calculator displays the digits 0, 1, 6, 8 and 9 so that, when the calculator is held upside-down, these digits appear to be 0, 1, 9, 8 and 6 respectively. Find the number of three-digit positive integers that look the same upside-down and right-side-up when using these five possible digits. (A three-digit string that begins with either "0" or "00" is not considered a three-digit positive integer.)

9. Find the number of non-congruent rectangles with integer sides that have no more than 25 square units in their areas.

10. Find the greatest possible range of a list of 5 distinct nonnegative integers with mean of 18 and median of 19.

Test 7. Sprint Round Problems

11. As shown in the figure, the solid is made of unit cubes and is hiding no holes. These cubes are rearranged to form a new rectangular solid. What is the smallest possible surface area of this new rectangular solid?

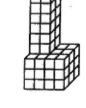

12. One of the vertices of a convex quadrilateral is at (2, −1). The other three vertices are at the reflections of (2, −1) about the x-axis, y-axis and the line $y = x$, respectively. Find the area of this quadrilateral.

13. One of the factors of 15^{90} is randomly chosen. Find the probability that the factor is a multiple of 15^{65}. Express your answer as a common fraction.

14. The perimeter of an isosceles triangle is 36 units and the altitude to the base is 12 units. Find the number of square units in its area.

15. The vertices of a pentagon points are at (0, 0), (1, 7), (6, 8), (10, 3), (2, 2) and (0, 0). Find the number of square units in the area of the pentagon.

16. As shown in the figure, $\triangle ABC$ is an isosceles right triangle with hypotenuse $\overline{AC}$. A circle is drawn through B that is tangent to $\overline{AC}$ at P. $\overline{PB}$ is a diameter of the circle. $\overline{AC} = 8$. Fin the number of square units are in the area of the region inside the circle but outside the triangle. Express your answer in terms of π.

17. Pedro has twelve more pencils than Peter. Paul has nine less pencils than Peter. Peter, Pedro and Paul decide to split the pencils so each of them will have the same number of pencils. Find the number of pencils Pedro will lose.

18. As shown in the figure, M and N are midpoints of legs $\overline{AB}$ and $\overline{BC}$ of right triangle ABC, respectively. $\overline{AB} = 6$ units. $\overline{BC} = 8$ units. Find the number of square units in the area of $\triangle APC$.

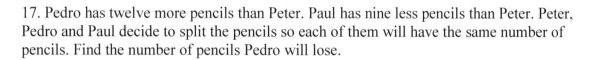

Test 7. Sprint Round Problems

19. The perimeter of a triangle is 80 inches. If the triangle's one side is 25 inches, find the fewest number of inches that can be the length of one of the remaining sides. All side lengths of the triangle are whole numbers.

20. Find the largest number c such that $2x^2 + 5x + c = 0$ has at least one real number solution. Express your answer as a common fraction.

21. Each of the boxes is replaced with a distinct number from $\{1, 2, 3, 4, 5, 6, 7, 8, 9\}$. Find the sum so that the sum is as close as possible to 1 without being greater than or equal to 1. Expressed your answer as a common fraction.

22. As shown in the figure, the points on a four-by-four grid are 1 unit apart horizontally and vertically. Two distinct points P and Q are selected at random from this grid. Find the probability that the distance between P and Q is less than 2.5. Express your answer as a common fraction.

23. As shown in the figure, a circle is inscribed in a quarter-circle. Find the radius r of the circle in terms of the radius R of the quarter-circle. Express the answer in simplest radical form.

24. Find the number of distinct triangles that can be constructed by connecting three different vertices of a cube.

25. As shown in the figure, circles Q and W are congruent and circle S and circle T are congruent. What is ratio of the areas of circle S to circle O?

26. The time needed for Franz to walk between her home and school is 45 minutes. She runs twice as fast as she walks. One morning she walked half way to school and realized

Test 7. Sprint Round Problems

that she forgot to bring her calculator. She ran home and it took 5 minutes at home to get her calculator. Then she ran all the way to school. How many minutes more than usual did it take her to get to school? Express your answer as a mixed number.

27. Find the area defined by the set of points (x, y) in the first quadrant which satisfy $3 \leq x + y \leq 5$.

28. Find the value of $n - m$ if $450 < n - m < 550$. n is a three-digit number and m is also a three-digit number obtained by interchanging the hundreds and units of n.

29. A regular tetrahedron is obtained by folding the piece shown below, with all indicated lengths of five units. Find the volume of the tetrahedron. Express your answer as a fraction in simplest radical form.

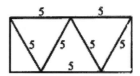

30. A four-digit positive integer has the property that the thousands digit equals the sum of the other three digits. Find the number of such four-digit positive integers greater than 5000.

Test 7. Target Round Problems

1. As shown in the figure, the home plate of a softball softball is a pentagon with three right angles. The other two angles of the home plate are congruent. Find the longest distance between any two vertices of this pentagon. Express the answer as a decimal to the nearest hundredths.

2. What is the value of the infinite geometric series $6 + 3.6 + 2.16 + 1.296 + \ldots$?

3. The positive integer 7 can be partitioned in many different ways. An example of a partition of 7 is $\{1, 1, 2, 3\}$, where 7 is the sum of one or more positive integers, with repetitions allowed. Find the probability that a randomly selected partition of 7 contains a prime number. Express your answer as a common fraction.

4. Find the fraction in the interval $\frac{7}{10} \leq x \leq \frac{8}{11}$ with the smallest denominator.

5. As shown in the figure, the square $SQUA$ has an area of 64 square units. M and N are the midpoints of sides SQ and SA, respectively. Find the number of square units in the area of the largest circle which can be drawn in pentagon $MNAUQ$. Express the answer to the nearest integer.

6. If two distinct points are selected randomly from the nine-point set $S = \{(1,1), (1,2), (1,3), (2,1), (2,2), (2,3), (3,1), (3,2), (3,3)\}$, find the probability that their midpoint belongs to S. Express your answer as a common fraction.

7. As shown in the figure, C is a point on the side BD of the rectangle $ABDE$. $\overline{AC} \perp \overline{CE}$, $BC = 4$ mm and $CD = 9$ mm. Find the number of millimeters in the length of $\overline{CE}$. Express your answer to the nearest integer.

8. Dr. Martinez leased a car for 3 years and drove the car 55, 240 miles. She needed to pay $1200 down and $299 per month for the length of the lease. In addition, she had to pay $0.15 per mile for all miles driven in excess of 45,000. Find the total number of dollars in the cost of the lease.

Test 8. Sprint Round Problems

1. Find the number of hours it will take to cook 672 hamburgers if eight hamburgers can be cooked every 5 minutes.

2. As shown in the figure, the side lengths of the triangle are 5, 6, and x. Find the positive difference between the greatest and least possible integral values of x.

3. The five-digit number 47, __ 21 is divisible by 3. Find the sum of all possible digits which could fill in the blank.

4. Find the value of $f(8) + f(2\sqrt{2})$ if $f(x)$ is defined by $f(x) = x^{\frac{2}{3}} - x^2$.

5. Find the number of centimeters in the perimeter of an isosceles triangle whose height is 12 cm and area 24 sq cm. Express your answer in simplest radical form.

6. Find the exponent of 10 when $4^{12} \times 5^{20}$ is written in scientific notation.

7. Three dimensions of a cereal box are increased by 20%. Find the percent by which the volume is increased. Express your answer rounded to the nearest whole number.

8. One jar contains 49% purple n&n's. A second jar contains 60% purple n&n's. The second jar contains 50% as many n&n' as the first jar. The contents of the two jars are mixed together. Find the percent of the n&n's in the mixture that are purple. Express your answer as a mixed number.

9. Two slices of bread can be put at once in a broken toaster but the toaster toasts only one side. So the bread must be flipped over to toast the other side. Find the least number of minutes required to toast five slices of bread on both sides if it takes 45 seconds to toast one side. Express your answer as a mixed number.

10. As shown in the figure, the area of the shaded region is 71 square meters. Find the number of square meters in the area of the larger of the two inner squares. All dimensions are positive integers.

11. A rectangle has the length and width of 3 cm and 4 cm, respectively. A square is formed by using a diagonal of the rectangle as a side. Then, a circle is circumscribed about the square. Find the number of square cm in the area of the circle. Express your answer as a common fraction in terms of π.

Test 8. Sprint Round Problems

12. Some, all, or none of right triangles with legs of length 1 unit are cut off the four corners of a rectangle. The dimensions of the rectangle are 2.5 units by 6 units. How many different shapes can be made with the cut including the original rectangle?

13. A rectangular aquarium measures 16 inches long, 9 inches wide, and 10 inches tall. It is filled with water to a level of 8 inches. A solid steel cube with an edge of 3 inches is dropped into the aquarium. Find the height of the new water level in the aquarium. Express your answer as a decimal rounded to the nearest tenth.

14. Find the result of $1 - 3 + 5 - 7 + 9 - 11 \ldots + 1993 - 1995 + 1997$. The expression is formed by alternately adding and subtracting consecutive odd integers starting with 1 and ending with 1997.

15. Find the number of square units in the area of $\triangle ABC$. The vertices of the triangle are located at the points $A(-5, 5)$, $B(2, 6)$ and $C(-2, 2)$ in a coordinate plane.

16. In a three-digit positive integer, the digit 5 is either the tens digit, the units digit, or both. How many such three-digit positive integers are there?

17. If Nancy gives Bill $10 instead, Bill has twice as much as Nancy. If Bill gives Nancy $10, they have the same amount of money. Find the sum of their money.

18. Big Kahuna, Major Domo, Em See, Lou Tenant and Captain Marv EL will occupy the five chairs arranged in a row. Major Domo cannot sit next to Big Kahuna. Find the number of possible seating arrangements.

19. The radius of circle O is 12 inches. $\triangle ABC$ is an equilateral triangle inscribed in circle O. Find the number of square inches in the area of $\triangle ABC$. Express your answer in simplest radical form.

20. Line segment $\overline{AB}$ with endpoints $A(-1, 2)$ and $B(5, 5)$ is reflected over the y-axis. The new image is reflected over the x-axis. Find the product of the coordinates of the midpoint of the final image.

21. Find the sum of the elements of A if $A = \{\frac{n}{24} | n$ is a natural number, $GCD(n, 24) = 1$, and $\frac{n}{24} < 2\}$.

22. Find the 280th letter in the sequence $A, A, B, A, B, C, A, B, C, D, A, B, C, D, E, \ldots$

Test 8. Sprint Round Problems

The above sequence was formed by writing the first letter of the alphabet followed by writing the first two letters of the alphabet and continuing the pattern by writing one more letter of the alphabet each time.

23. The front face of a rectangular prism has a 13 inches long diagonal and a 5 inches long height. The top face of the same prism has a 15 inches long diagonal. Find the number of cubic inches in the volume of the prism. Each of the dimensions is an integer length.

24. When the 50th term of the harmonic sequence $\frac{1}{2}, \frac{1}{4}, \frac{1}{6}, \cdots$ is divided by the nth term, the quotient is 4. Find the value of n. A harmonic sequence is a sequence of numbers in which the reciprocals form an arithmetic sequence.

25. John ordered ordered 4 CD's and some additional tapes. The price of a CD was double the price of a tape. When the order arrived, the number of CDs had been interchanged with the number of tapes. The bill was 50% more than he expected. Find the number of tapes John ordered originally.

26. As shown in the figure, each of the digits 1, 2, 3, . . ., and 9 is arranged in a circle, in the triangle. The sum of the numbers on each side of the triangle is the same. Find the positive difference between the greatest and least sums possible.

27. Point A has coordinates (3, 11) and point B has coordinates (18, 1). Point P is on $\overline{AB}$. The ratio of $AP : PB = 2 : 3$. Find the sum of the coordinates of point P.

28. Find the greatest integral solution of $|x-5| > |2x-5|$.

29. Two different numbers are selected at random from the set of integers greater than 0 and less than 9. Find the probability that they have no common prime factor. Express your answer as a common fraction.

30. Find a positive integer such that 5^{96} is greater than n^{72} and 5^{96} is less than $(n+1)^{72}$.

Test 8. Target Round Problems

1. What is the area of the region determined by the system of inequalities? Express your answer as a decimal.

$$x - y \leq 4$$
$$x \geq -1$$
$$x \leq 3$$
$$x \geq -4$$
$$y \leq 5$$

2. The length is 12 inches and the width is 8 inches of a rectangular piece of sheet metal One square piece of 1.5 inches by 1.5 inches is cut from each corner. The sheet is then folded to form an open rectangular box. Find the number of cubic inches in the volume of the box. Express your answer as a decimal to the nearest tenth.

3. The outside radius is 1.7 inches and the inside radius is 1.5 inches of a hollow piece of cylindrical pipe. Find the number of square inches in the total surface area of the pipe if it is 3 feet long. Express your answer as a decimal to the nearest tenth.

4. The overall mean score was 82 of the 25 students in a test. The mean score of the 12 boys was 75. Find the mean score of the girls in the class. Express your answer rounded to the nearest tenth.

5. An integer is selected randomly from 0 and 5000 inclusive. It is found that the integer selected to be a perfect cube. Find the probability that it is also a perfect fourth power. Express your answer as a common fraction.

6. As shown in the figure, a circular field had a radius of 120 feet. Pedro stood at the center of the field at first. He walked due north halfway to the circle. He then turned and walked due east halfway to the circle. He turned again and walked due south halfway to the circle. Finally, he turned and walked due west halfway to the circle. Find the number of feet Pedro was from the center of the circle when he stopped. Express your answer to the nearest foot

7. 6000 apples were harvested. It was found that every third apple was too small, every fourth apple was too green, and every tenth apple was bruised. The rest were perfect. How many perfect apples were harvested?

8. A sidewalk with a uniform width of 25 feet surrounded a circular garden. The total area of the garden is the same as the total area of the sidewalk. Find the diameter of the garden in feet. Round your answer to the nearest integer.

Test 9. Sprint Round Problems

1. As shown in the figure, $\triangle ABC$ is isosceles with $AB = BC$. Find the number of degrees in the measure of $\angle B$.

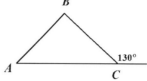

2. Find the number of positive integers divisors of 225225.

3. Find the percent increase of a positive number from 4.00 to 4.50. Express your answer to the nearest tenth of a percent.

4. Clock A loses 30 seconds a day. Clock B gains 45 seconds a day. Clock B is 10 minutes behind ahead of clock A now. Find the number of days it will take for clock B to be 5 minutes ahead of clock A.

5. Joe's home is in Albuquerque. He needs to visit Baltimore, Cleveland, Denver and Evanston, in no particular order. In how many different ways can he travel from Albuquerque to each of the other cities, and return to Albuquerque, without visiting any of the other four cities more than once?

6. As shown in the figure, each box is filled with a different prime number. No two adjacent boxes hold numbers that differ by 2. The sum of all nine primes is as small as possible. Find the sum of the nine primes.

7. As shown in the figure, a large circle with successively smaller inscribed equilateral triangles and circles. The smallest circle has the area of 4π square meters. Find the number of square meters in the area of the largest circle. Express your answer in terms of π.

8. Find the number of even four-digit positive integers greater than 7000 that can be formed using the digits 3, 4, 5, 7 and 9. No repetition of digits is allowed in a number.

Test 9. Sprint Round Problems

9. If three green marbles are removed from a bag containing only blue and green marbles, the probability of drawing a green marble from the remaining marbles is $\frac{2}{5}$. If, instead, seven blue marbles are added to the bag, the probability of drawing a blue marble is $\frac{5}{8}$. Find the number of blue marbles in the bag originally.

10. Find the units digit in the product $3^1 \cdot 3^2 \cdot 3^2 \cdot 3^2 \cdots 3^{99} \cdot 3^{100}$ where all the whole number powers of 3 from 3^1 to 3^{100} inclusive are multiplied.

11. Brendon gave $\frac{5}{7}$ of his money to his brother. His brother spent $\frac{5}{7}$ of that and returned the remaining money to Brendon. The remaining amount was $40 less than the amount Brendon had left. How many dollars did Brendon have originally?

12. As shown in the figure, the large circle in the center is tangent to all four semicircles, and the semicircles are all tangent to the quarter-circles. The circle, semicircles and quarter-circles each have a radius of 4 miles. Find the number of square miles in the area of the shaded region. Express your answer in terms of π.

13. The Wonderlich family has three children and at least one of them is female Find the probability that at least one of the three children is a male. Having a male of female child is equally likely.

14. Find the greatest possible value for $a + b$ if $a^2 + 2ab + b^2 = 144$.

15. Chen and Elyes will have the same amount of money if Chen gives Elyes $5. Chen will have three times as much as Elyse has if Elyse gives Chen $5. Find the sum of their money.

16. The sum of of weights of three dogs is 185 pounds. The two smaller dogs weigh the same. The difference is 20 pounds between the larger weight and the smaller weight. Find the weight in pounds of the largest dog.

17. The side of an equilateral triangle is 8 inches long. If the altitude of this triangle is used as a side of a square, find the number of square inches in the area of the square.

18. The total distance Elizabeth biked on a 6-day trip was 504 miles. On each day n of the trip, she biked n times as many miles as she biked on the first day. (For example, on day

Test 9. Sprint Round Problems

4, she biked four times as many miles as she had on the first day.) Find the distance she biked on the first day.

19. As shown in the figure, the lengths indicated on the rectangle are in centimeters. Find the number of square centimeters in the area of the shaded region.

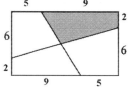

20. A positive integer less than 200 has exactly 9 divisors. Find sum of all the positive integers with this property.

21. The positive difference of two positive integers is two less than their sum. Find the product of the least two such positive integers.

22. If each side of a square is decreased by 25%, the area of the square will decreases by 7 square meters. Find the number of square meters in the area of the original square.

23. Find the product of the 4th and the 1998th terms of an arithmetic sequence given that the third term is 5 and the eighth term is –20.

24. Each of the letters of the word MATHCOUNTS is written on one card. These ten cards are placed in a basket. Two cards are picked randomly without replacement. Find the probability that the first card chosen has a vowel on it and the second card chosen has a consonant. Express your answer as a common fraction.

25. The ratio of the lengths of the corresponding sides of two similar triangles is 2 : 3. The area of the smaller triangle is 100 square feet. Find the number of square feet in the area of the larger triangle.

26. As shown in the figure, equilateral triangles are formed by connection the midpoints of the sides of other equilateral triangles. Find the area of the shaded portion of the figure if each side of the largest triangle is 12 inches long. Express your answer as a common fraction in simplest radical form.

27. The perimeter of a rectangle is 44 centimeters. Two diagonals intersect at point P which is 5 centimeters further from the shorter side than the longer side. Find the area of the rectangle.

Test 9. Sprint Round Problems

28. $\triangle ABC$ is a scalene triangle with one side 3 centimeters and second side 5 centimeters. Find the number of different whole number centimeter lengths possible for the third side.

29. The sum of Great Aunt Minnie's age and the square of Great Uncle Paul's age is 7308. The sum of Great Uncle Paul's age and the square of Great Aunt Minnie's age is 6974. Find the sum of Great Aunt Minnie's age and Great Uncle Paul's age.

30. Alan, Beth and Cindy put their money to purchase lottery tickets. Alan invested $25.00, Beth invested $20.00, and Cindy invested $35.00. The winnings totaled 6.4 million dollars. Find the number of dollars Beth's share of the winnings. The amount received was proportional to the amount invested.

Test 9. Target Round Problems

1. Calculate:

$$\frac{1}{1+\dfrac{1}{1+\dfrac{1}{1+1}}} + \frac{2}{2+\dfrac{2}{2+\dfrac{2}{2+2}}}$$

Express your answer as a common fraction.

2. As shown in the figure, a 4″ × 6″ × 8″ rectangular solid is cut by slicing through the midpoints of three adjacent sides. Find the number of inches in the sum of the lengths of the edges of the tetrahedron that is cut. Express your answer as a decimal rounded to the nearest tenth.

3. Three players are required to play the game of *Rock, Paper, Scissors.* Each player shows either four finagles (Paper), two fingers (Scissors) or a fist (Rock) at the same time. Find the probability that exactly two players show the same sign. Express your answer as a common fraction.

4. It took 0.4 seconds for the ball to travel a distance of 60′6″ from the pitcher's mound to home plate. Find the speed of the ball in miles per hour. Express your answer rounded to the nearest whole number.

5. As shown in the figure, E is the midpoint of $\overline{AB}$, D is the midpoint of $\overline{AC}$, $AB = 16$ cm. $AC = 12$ cm. Find the number of square centimeters in the area of pentagon $AEFGD$.

6. Tom got his lowest score on the fourth test of five math tests. He got an integer score on each of the five tests. He never scored higher than 90. If his average score, rounded to the nearest integer, was 82, find the lowest possible score he could have earned on the fourth test.

7. There are a total of 21 questions in a science test. Among them, 10 questions worth 5 points each, 7 questions worth 6 points each, and 4 questions worth 2 points each. None of these questions will be given partial credit. How many scores between 0 and 100 are impossible to get?

Test 9. Target Round Problems

8. As shown in the figure, the radius of the large semicircle is 1 centimeter, and the radius of the small circle is 0.5 centimeters. If the length of the longer leg on the right triangle is 3 centimeters, find the number of square centimeters in the area that is not shaded in the diagram. Use 3.14 as an approximation for π. Express your answer as a decimal rounded to the nearest tenth.

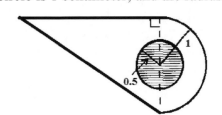

Test 10. Sprint Round Problems

1. A positive three-digit integer is selected at random from all the positive three-digit integers formed using the digits 0, 2, 4, 6, and 8 without repetition. Find the probability that the positive three-digit integer is divisible by 3. The first digit cannot be 0 in any of these positive three-digit integer. Express your answer as a common fraction.

2. A fly walks from one vertex of a cube with edge length 1 inch along edges of the cube. Find the number of inches in the longest distance that it could walk without retracing any edge.

3. A jar contains four red balls and two white balls. One ball is removed at random and replaced with a ball of the opposite color. Then one ball is randomly selected. Find the probability that this ball is red. Express your answer as a common fraction.

4. The ratio of girls to boys was 2 : 3 after one-fifth of the girls left a school dance. Then, 44 boys left and the ratio of boys to girls was 2 : 5. Find the number of students remained at the dance.

5. As shown in the figure, $ABCD$ is a square with $AB = 2$ cm. Points E and F are midpoints of $\overline{AD}$ and $\overline{DC}$, respectively. Find the number of square centimeters in the area of $\triangle BEF$. Express your answer as a common fraction.

6. Three cards are dealt randomly without replacement from 8 red and 7 black cards. Find the probability that the three cards dealt are the same color. Express your answer as a common fraction.

7. Find the maximum possible number of points of intersection of two circles and three straight lines lie in the same plane.

8. Find the area of a triangle whose sides measure 8 cm, 12 cm and 16 cm. Express your answer in simplest radical form.

9. A cube with edge length 9 inches is circumscribed about a sphere. A smaller cube is inscribed in the sphere. Find the volume of the smaller cube. Express your answer in simplest radical form.

Test 10. Sprint Round Problems

10. As shown in the figures, stage 1 is obtained by dividing the area in state 0 into four congruent squares and the lower right square of the four is shaded. Find the fractional part of the square in stage 3 that will be shaded if the pattern continues. Express your answer as a common fraction.

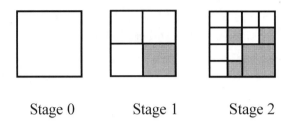

Stage 0   Stage 1   Stage 2

11. As shown in the figure, $\triangle ABC$ is an equilateral triangle. $AB = 2$ meters. Points A, B and C are centers of circles whose radii are 1 meter. Find the shaded area. Express your answer as a decimal to the nearest hundredth.

12. Find the smallest value of x such that $|5x - 1| = |3x + 2|$? Express your answer as a common fraction.

13. Find the value of $(f^{-1}(1))^{-1}$. $f(x) = \dfrac{4x+1}{3}$.

14. As shown in the figure, $AB = BC = AD = x + 8$, and $CD = 3x - 9$. Find the sum of the smallest and largest possible integer values of x.

15. A circle has the diameter of 26 centimeters. Find the length of a chord whose midpoint is 12 cm from the center of the circle.

16. Find the sum of all positive two-digit integers with exactly 12 positive factors.

Test 10. Sprint Round Problems

17. As shown in the figure, $ABCD$ is a square. $AD = 4$ centimeters. M is the midpoint of $\overline{CD}$. Find the ratio of OC to OA. Express your answer as a common fraction.

18. A palindrome is a number that reads the same forward and backward, such as 313. Find the probability that a randomly selected three-digit positive integer is a palindrome. Express our answer as a common fraction.

19. Two positive integers are relatively prime and each is less than 20. Find the sum of them if their product minus their sum is 39.

20. A fraction is equivalent to $\frac{9}{10}$. When 8 is subtracted from the numerator and denominator of the fraction, the result was a fraction equivalent to $\frac{5}{6}$. Find the sum of the numerator and denominator of the original fraction.

21. Fifteen balls are labeled 1–15, with each ball one label. Four balls are selected randomly without replacement. Find the probability that the sum of the numbers on those four balls is odd. Express your answer as a common fraction.

22. Find the total number of squares in the figure.

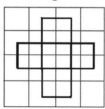

23. When a positive integer is divided by 7, the remainder of 5. Find the remainder when the same positive integer is by 5 and then divides by 7.

24. A triangle has one side 7 centimeters and second side 12 centimeters. A number is chosen at random from the first twenty positive integers 1, 2, 3, . . . , 20. Find the probability that the number chosen could be the length in centimeters of the third side. Express your answer as a common fraction.

Test 10. Sprint Round Problems

25. Two digits are placed in the two boxes below (one for the hundreds and one for the units digits). The resulting five-digit number is the smallest possible and divisible by 36. Find the ratio of the smaller digit to the larger digit. Express your answer as a common fraction.

26. An arithmetic sequence consists of positive integers. The sum of the first ten terms of this arithmetic sequence is always divisible by a positive integer m. Find the greatest value for m.

27. Four squares are shown in the figure. Find the shaded region. The side length of each square is 1 centimeter. The shaded region is formed by two parallel segments connecting the midpoints of congruent squares. Express your answer as a common fraction.

28. Find the value of $(f(f(-2)))^{-2}$. $f(x) = \dfrac{1}{1 - \dfrac{1}{1 - \dfrac{1}{1-x}}}$. Express your answer as a common fraction.

29. A second equilateral triangle is formed by connecting the midpoints of the three sides of an equilateral triangle. A third triangle is formed by connection the midpoints of the second triangle. Find the ratio of the perimeter of the tenth triangle to the perimeter of the third triangle if the process is repeated. Express your answer as a common fraction.

30. As shown in the figure, each square has the side length 1 centimeter long. Each row contains one more square than the row above it. Find the perimeter of the figure formed by arranging 210 squares in this fashion.

Test 10. Target Round Problems

1. A three-digit number is obtained when a two-digit number is multiplied by 5. If the digit 7 is written after the resulting three-digit number, the new four-digit number is 1281 greater than the original two-digit number. Find the original number.

2. A sign in a city indicates the amount of money Americans had saved using one phone company instead of another. At 3:50 pm on January 1, 1999, the sign read $2,519,206,712. The sign adds $1 each 0.1 seconds. . Find the month and year the sign will read $9,999,999,999.

3. If the perimeter of a semicircle is numerically the same as its area, find the radius of the semicircle. Express your answer as a decimal to the nearest hundredth.

4. $A(2, 4)$, $B(6, 4)$ and $C(4, 10)$ are three vertices of $\triangle ABC$ in a coordinate plane. Find the sum of the abscissas of the coordinates of the vertices be when $\triangle ABC$ is reflected over the line $x = 8$.

5. It took Mark 3 minutes to run the first half of a one-mile race. During the third quarter of the race, his speed was 8 mph, and, during the final quarter, his speed was only $\frac{3}{5}$ of his speed during the first half. Find his average speed for the entire race in miles per hour, Express your answer as a decimal to the nearest tenth.

6. The surface of a $4'' \times 4'' \times 4''$ cube is painted. It is then cut into sixty-four $1'' \times 1'' \times 1''$ cubes. One of the $1'' \times 1'' \times 1''$ cubes is then selected at random and rolled. Find the probability that the top face of the rolled cube is painted. Express your answer as a common fraction.

7. As shown in the figure, $AB = 150$ cm, $CD = 100$ cm. $\overline{AB} \parallel \overline{CD} \parallel \overline{EF}$. Find the number of centimeters in the length of $\overline{EF}$.

8. As shown in the figure, $CABD$ is a semicircular path. Diameter $\overline{CD}$ has length 180 m. Find the number of meters of distance Marcia will save if she walks along chord AB instead of arc AB. Express your answer as a decimal to the nearest tenth.

Test 11. Sprint Round Problems

1. Find the greatest possible product of the two primes whose sum is 29.

2. The sum of the square of Winslow's age and Abby's age is 209. The sum of the square of Abby's age and Winslow's age is 183. Find the sum of their ages.

3. Solve the equation for xs $\dfrac{0.\overline{09}}{x} = 11^{-1}$.

4. As shown in the figure, A, B and C are three vertices of a cube. Find the area of $\triangle ABC$ if the volume of the cube is 27 cubic inches. Express your answer as a fraction in simplest radical form.

5. Alex wants to create one–digit or two–digit numbers with 8 each of the digits 1–8. How many different numbers he can make at most?

6. Seven positive integers have a median of 73, a mode of 79, and a mean of 75. Find the least possible difference between the maximum and minimum values of these seven integers.

7. Find the thirteenth term of an arithmetic sequence if the third term is –1 and the ninth term is 20.

8. Find the number of integer values of x such that $x^2 + 2x - 19$ is less than zero.

9. Find the value of $m - n$ if m is the number of positive integer factors of 876,876, and n is the number of positive integer factor of 678,678.

10. As shown in the figure, the magic square consists of the positive integers 1-25 such that the sum of the numbers in any row, any column, and any diagonal is the same. Find the value of n.

	24	1	8	15
23		7	14	16
4	6	13		
10	12	n	21	3
		25		9

11. *Palindromic primes* are prime numbers that read the same backwards and forwards. For example, 101 ia a palindromic prime. Find the sum of all palindromic primes between 100 and 200.

Test 11. Sprint Round Problems

12. A fair six-sided number cube with the digits 1-6 on its faces is rolled three times. The positive difference between the values on the first two rolls is equal to the value of the third roll. What is the probability that at least one 3 was rolled? Express your answer as a common faction.

13. The product of a two-digit number and 5 is equal to the product of the same two-digit number with its digits reversed and 6. What is the sum of the digits of the number?

14. A box contains five balls numbered 1, 2, 3, 4 and 5. Three balls are drawn at random without replacement. What is the probability that the median of the values on the three chosen balls is greater than 2? Express your answer as a common fraction.

15. What is the number of centimeters in the perimeter of the rhombus shown?

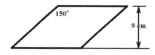

16. What is the largest integer value of n for which 8^n evenly divides 100! ?

17. In $\triangle ABC$, $\angle C$ is a right angle. Point M is the midpoint of $\overline{AB}$, point N is the midpoint of $\overline{AC}$, and point O is the midpoint of $\overline{AM}$. The perimeter of $\triangle ABC$ is 112 cm, and $ON = 12.5$ cm. What is the number of square centimeters in the area of quadrilateral $MNCB$?

18. In each of three boxes are four straws with integer lengths 1 cm through 4cm, inclusive. A straw is randomly selected from each box. What is the probability that a triangle can be formed with the three straws chosen? Express your answer as a common fraction.

19. Alyssa rode her bicycle for seven hours. She started on level ground and rode at a rate of 8 mph. She came to a hill that slowed her down to a rate of 5 mph. Upon reaching the top of the hill, she turned around and descended at a rate of 20 mph. Finally, she returned home on the flat portion at 8 mph. What is the total number of miles that she rode?

20. The probability of drawing a red marble from a jar of marbles is $\frac{1}{5}$. If three marbles are drawn with replacement, what is the probability that none of the marbles drawn is red? Express your answer as a common fraction.

Test 11. Sprint Round Problems

21. Moves are only allowed one segment to the right or one segment up. How many paths from A to B are possible?

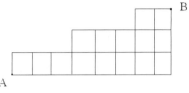

22. Compute: $100^2 - 99^2 + 98^2 - 97^2 + 96^2 - \ldots - 1^2$.

23. What is the sum of the three numbers less than 1000 that have exactly five positive integer divisors?

24. Ellen has five different jobs to be done. She assigns all five jobs to her four kids. Each kid will have at least one job. How many ways can Ellen assign the jobs?

25. What is the value of the following expression?

$$\sqrt{6+\sqrt{6+\sqrt{6+\sqrt{6+\ldots}}}}$$

26. A diagonal of a rectangle is 41 inches, and the perimeter is 98 inches. What is the number of square inches in the area of the rectangle?

27. The product of a set of positive integers is 144. What is the least possible sum of this set of positive integers?

28. The Sagebrush student council has 6 boys and 6 girls as class representatives. Two different subcommittees, each consisting of 2 boys and 2 girls, are to be created. If no student can serve on both subcommittees, how many different combinations of subcommittees are possible?

29. Sarah is reading a newspaper when she realizes that four numbered pages of one section are missing. If one of the missing pages is numbered 9 and there are 40 pages in the section, what is the sum of the other three missing page numbers?

30. For positive integers a, b and c, what is the value of the product abc?

$$\cfrac{1}{a+\cfrac{1}{b+\cfrac{1}{c}}} = \frac{3}{8}.$$

Test 11. Target Round Problems

1. The sum of the quotient of two positive integers and the reciprocal of their quotient is 2.9. Find the product of the two integers if their sum is 56.

2. A type of algae grows continuously and its population doubles in 3 days. If the beginning population is 100 algae cells per milliliter of water, find the number of algae cells per milliliter at the end of 10 days. Express your answer to the nearest whole number.

3. It takes 35 minutes for Megan to bike to school but walk home. The time needed for Megan to bike the round-trip is 30 minutes less than the time needed for Megan to walk the round-trip. Find the number of minutes it takes for Megan to walk one way.

4. As shown in the figure, three points are selected at random from the nine equally-spaced points. Find the probability that these three points form an isosceles triangle. Express your answer as a common fraction.

5. The number 987654321098765. . . 543210 is a 200-digit number. This number repeats the digits 0-9 in reverse order. Choose every third digit from the left to right to form a new number. Repeat the same process with the new number. Continue the process until a two-digit number is obtained. Find this two-digit number.

6. As shown in the figure, each of the four circles is tangent to other two. The four circles are also are tangent to an external square. A smaller circle is drawn tangent to each of the larger circles. Find the number of square centimeters in the area of the smaller circle if the radius of the larger circle is 4 cm. Express your answer as a decimal to the nearest tenth.

7. Find the sum of all real numbers x satisfying the following equation:
$(x^2 - 5x + 5)^{(x^2 - 7x + 12)} = 1$?

8. A bag contains some blue and green marbles. Two marbles are selected at random without replacement. The probability that they are both blue is $\frac{1}{6}$. If three marbles are selected at random without replacement, the probability that all three are blue is $\frac{1}{21}$. Find the fewest number of the marbles that must have been in the bag originally.

Made in the USA
Middletown, DE
04 February 2018